SELF-STUDY BOOK

by Sheelagh Deller

HEINEMANN

Contents

Introduction 1

unit 1	Starting a New Course	2
unit 2	People and Customs	6
unit 3	Selling Yourself	10
unit 4	Memories and Experiences	16
unit 5	Food and Entertainment	20
unit 6	Legal and Illegal	25
unit 7	Our Surroundings	30
unit 8	Education	34
unit 9	How it Works	38
unit 10	Looking into the Future	42
unit 11	Transport and Travel	46
unit 12	Learning English — Looking Backwards and Forwards	50

Key 54

Heinemann International,
a division of Heinemann Publishers (Oxford) Ltd,
Halley Court, Jordan Hill, Oxford OX2 8EJ

OXFORD LONDON EDINBURGH
MADRID ATHENS BOLOGNA PARIS
MELBOURNE SYDNEY AUCKLAND SINGAPORE TOKYO
IBADAN NAIROBI HARARE GABORONE
PORTSMOUTH (NH)

ISBN 0 435 28186 0

© Sheelagh Deller 1992

All rights reserved; no part of this publication may be reproduced, stored in a retrieval system, or transmitted in any form or by any means, electronic, mechanical, photocopying, recording, or otherwise, without the prior permission of the publishers.
First published 1992

Cover by Andrew Oliver
Designed by Andrew Oliver

Typeset by Pentacor PLC, High Wycombe, Bucks

Printed and bound in Great Britain by
Thomson Litho Ltd, East Kilbride, Glasgow.

92 93 94 95 96 97 10 9 8 7 6 5 4 3 2 1

Introduction

The main objectives of this book are
1. to give you the opportunity to work on your own on areas that are important for you
2. to extend your vocabulary
3. to help you with some of the peculiarities of English pronunciation
4. to enjoy yourself at the same time as improving your English

- This book is closely linked with the **Vista** Coursebook in terms of topics and language points covered. As such it is a useful support for you to work on your own on areas that you are not yet confident about. You may not have time to do all the activities, so you can pick and choose the ones which will be most useful for you.
- In addition there is new material focusing on pronunciation and more vocabulary.
- The key to all the activities is at the end of the book so you can check your own work as you go along.
- Some of the exercises are recorded on the **Vista** cassettes. All the answers are in the key so you can use the book without the cassettes. However, the recordings are there to add to your enjoyment and understanding of some of the reading passages and all the poems, and to help you with the pronunciation work. The recorded material is marked with the symbol.

Organisation

There are twelve units each on the same topic as the corresponding units in **Vista** Coursebook. However, the sections within the units are slightly different. Each unit has separate sections (but not necessarily in the following order) for Reading, Writing, Pronunciation, Vocabulary, and Language Focus (grammar). Each unit starts with a humorous quotation related to the topic, and ends with a poem.

Pronunciation

At your level your pronunciation needs may be very individual. For this reason there is not much work on pronunciation in the **Vista** Coursebook, but there is a section on it in every unit of the Self-study Book. Pronunciation work can be less embarrassing and more effective when you work on it by yourself. The pronunciation sections cover activities to work on sound level, word level and sentence level. The poems at the end of each section can give further pronunciation practice for stress, rhythm and intonation. All the pronunciation work is recorded on the cassettes. If you don't have copies of these you could ask your teacher to play you the relevant parts in class. In addition, all the answers are in the key so you can still use the book even if you don't have the cassettes.

Vocabulary

Another aspect of the Self-study Book which is 'extra' to the Coursebook is further vocabulary work. This includes vocabulary areas related to particular themes and also activities on synonyms and the appropriacy of different words or phrases for different purposes. There are also generative activities, for example on understanding the effects of different prefixes and suffixes.

Poems

Each unit ends with a poem. These range from classical to modern. Some are serious, some humorous. They are included primarily for your enjoyment. Poetry is often difficult to understand, even in our own language. Treat the poems in this book as pleasure not pain. Don't be put off if you don't understand every line. Just enjoy them, and work on your pronunciation by reading them aloud to yourself and listening to the sounds of the words.

Acknowledgements

The publishers would like to thank the following for their kind permission to use their material in this book: African Universities Press for 'Telephone Conversation', p15 by Wole Soyinka; Carcanet Press Ltd for Spacepoem 3: Off Course, p45 by Edwin Morgan from *Collected Poems*; Complete Editions for the tongue-twisters, pp4, 8, 19, 41, 49, 53 from *The Crazy Encyclopedia* by Gyles Brandreth, Transworld 1981; Andre Deutsch Ltd for the quotes from George Mikes, p6 and from Robert Benchley, p2; Diagram Visual Information Ltd for material, pp38, 43 from *How to hold a Crocodile* (Sidgwick and Jackson 1981); Peter Dixon for 'I'd like to be a teabag', p10; Faber and Faber Ltd for 'Macavity the Mystery Cat' p29 from *Old Possum's Book of Practical Cats* by T S Eliot; Georgia Garrett for 'Manwatching', p9 (originally published in *I See a Voice* by Michael Rosen, Thames TV); Harper Collins Publishers Ltd for puzzles, p8 and anagrams, p9 from *Word for Word* by Ronald Ridout; Robert Luff Ltd and Lenny Henry for the questionnaire, p6 from *The Correspondent* Magazine; New Harbinger for 'Twenty things I love to do', p42 from *Thoughts and Feelings*, McKay et al; Penguin Books Ltd for 'From the Files of Inspector Craig', p27 from *What's the name of this book?* by Raymond Smullyan, 'On the Motivation to Work,' p12 from 'Understanding Organizations' by Charles B Handy; Peters Fraser & Dunlop Group Ltd for 'Vegetarians', p24 from *Holiday on Death Row* by Roger McGough (Jonathan Cape); 'The Proper Study', p37 by W S Slater reproduced with permission of Punch; Reader's Digest Association Ltd. © 1973 for the recipe for Cold Caramel Soufflé, p20; Scholastic Publications Ltd for 'Spell it', p35 from *When did you last wash your feet?* by Michael Rosen; Rogers, Coleridge & White Ltd for 'Mother Nature Awards' by Miles Kington, p30; 'On Time for Once', p53 from *Love Poems* by Brian Patten (Paladin, first published 1981) and 'Someone stole the ', p18 from *Gargling with Jelly* by Brian Patten (Viking Kestrel 1985); The Sunday Telegraph Ltd/Alan Sutton Publishing Ltd for 'The Shortest Story', p17;

All our efforts at tracing the copyright holder of 'Problem Child' p5 by J E Faulks, have been unsuccessful, and we would be interested to hear from any copyright holders not acknowledged.

Illustrated by Shirley Barker pp15, 37; Caroline Church pp41, 49; Diane Fisher p30; Peter Hudspith pp5, 6, 10, 24; Andrew Oliver p8; Rodney Shackell pp29, 47; Gary Wing pp2, 9, 26, 45.

unit 1

Starting a New Course

'Drawing on my fine command of language, I said nothing.'
Robert Benchley (1889–1945), American humorous editor, critic, actor and author.

Language Focus

1 Complete the following sentences with information about yourself. Include a verb in each of your answers.

a Before I came on this course ....
....

b At the moment I'm ....
....

c I wish I could ....
....

d I've never ....
....

e I'm determined to ....
....

f For the last two years ....
....

g On Saturdays I ....
....

h When I was eleven I couldn't stand ....
....

i I'm really good ....
....

j I'm hopeless ....
....

k I enjoy ....
....

l I can't bear ....
....

2

a Look at the information about Marco and complete the **me** column in the same way with information about yourself.

	Marco	Me
What I've done in the last five years.	learn drive visit USA buy house	
What I did before that.	university live with parents ride bicycle	
What I'm doing now.	work newspaper study English live alone	

b Now read the paragraph about Marco and write a paragraph in the same way about yourself.

In the last five years Marco has learnt to drive, he has visited the USA and he has bought a house. Before that he lived with his parents, went to university and rode a bicycle. At the moment he is working for a newspaper, studying English and living alone.

Reading

1 Fill each blank in these sentences with a suitable preposition.

Learning a Language

1 The reason (**a**) .... learning a foreign language is to be able to use it (**b**) .... communicate (**c**) .... people who don't speak our language.

2 The best way to learn another language is to use it rather (**a**) .... just talk (**b**) .... it. In this respect it's similar to learning to drive a car. You learn to drive (**c**) .... sitting in the driver's seat and having 'hands (**d**) ....' experience. (**e**) .... course, you also need to have some knowledge about the Highway Code and the way the car operates. The same is true (**f**) .... a foreign language.

3 Different people prefer different kinds (**a**) .... learning styles and strategies. If you really want to learn another language you will probably find the best way (**b**) .... you.

4 In your class you will be learning (**a**) .... your fellow-learners and your teacher. It will be a gradual process so don't expect too much (**b**) .... yourself.

5 Unless you intend to become an interpreter, there is no need or point (**a**) .... aiming to speak a foreign language like a native speaker. Your own language is a strong part (**b**) .... your make-up and will affect your use of a foreign language. This is good as it enables you (**c**) .... keep your own identity, even when you're using another language.

6 Language is more (**a**) .... just vocabulary and grammar. These are just the tools you have to express yourself (**b**) .... clearly as you can, in the way that suits you.

7 There will be a lot (**a**) .... exercises and activities in the classroom which will try to mirror life (**b**) .... the classroom.

8 Your coursebook is there (**a**) .... help you learn and to give you examples (**b**) .... language, and opportunities to practice. It's also useful (**c**) .... reference. But there may be parts of it that are not helpful or necessary for you. So you and your teacher can be selective and use this book (**d**) .... a starting point, rather (**e**) .... (**f**) .... a 'chore' that has to be totally digested.

9 Don't be afraid (**a**) .... making mistakes (**b**) .... a foreign language. Making mistakes is part (**c**) .... the learning process. If you want to enrich your use and knowledge of the language, and become more fluent, then you will need to take some risks. Your teacher will sometimes correct you (**d**) .... the time, and sometimes later (**e**) ....

10 Learning a foreign language is hard work, but should also be fun, (**a**) .... all, the objective is to be able to interact (**b**) .... other people, and feel comfortable and relaxed while doing so.

Writing

Choose the four statements about learning a language that interest you most.

unit 1

Vocabulary

1 Complete these staircases with the words from the lists. Put the strongest word on the top step. You can put more than one word on a step.

a Adjectives to express a reaction to something, for example, to a film

wonderful awful appalling fantastic terrible
superb okay bad all right good

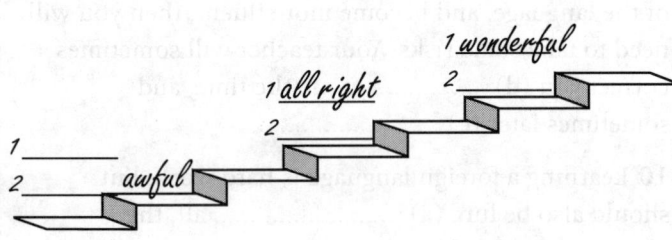

b Adjectives to express tiredness

tired sleepy shattered dozy exhausted
drowsy all in dead beat

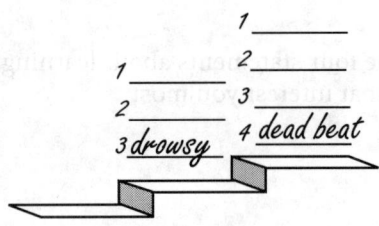

c Adjectives to describe degrees of wetness, for example, for clothes or a person

damp wet soaking dripping saturated
wet through

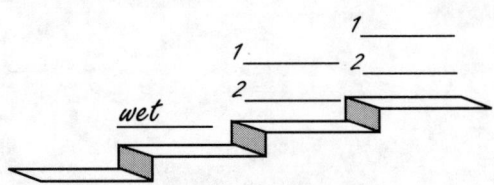

d Adjectives to express hunger

hungry peckish famished starving ravenous

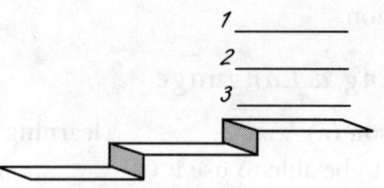

Pronunciation

1 Put these regular verbs into the past tense and then put them into the correct column below according to their final sound.

manage analyse introduce hate dislike
finish adore study receive adapt advise
attain focus react fail diagnose identify
manipulate perform describe depend stroke
pretend

/d/	/t/	/id/
managed	finished	hated

2 🔊

Say these words aloud and circle the odd one out. Add two more words that would fit in with the words you didn't circle.

our flower flour your hour ....

four sour soar more poor ....

hood food put stood foot ....

3 🔊

Say these tongue-twisters five times each as quickly as you can.

Pure food for poor mules.
Georgie's gorge is gorgeous.

4

Poem

1. You're going to read a poem about a young schoolboy. Before you read it try to guess which of the following activities he likes or dislikes and put ✓ in the appropriate column below.

	He likes it	He doesn't like it
Painting		
Dictation		
Spelling tests		
Self-expression		
Doing things		
Dodging things		
Projects		
Arithmetic		
Modelling		

2. Now read the poem and put in the correct information about what he likes and dislikes.

3. Read the poem aloud and notice the rhyming words.

Problem Child JE Faulks

How *shall* I deal with Roger,
    Mrs Prodger?
I've never yet been able
To sit him at a table
And make him paint a label
For the salmon in the kindergarten shop.
    But he's full of animation
    When I mention a dictation,
    And never wants a spelling-test to stop.
I've encouraged self-expression
And intentional digression
But I think I'll have to let the system drop.
    For the normal child, like Roger,
    Is a *do*-er, not a dodger,
And your methods, Mrs Prodger, are a flop.

How *shall* I deal with Roger,
    Mrs Prodger?
I've had projects on the fairies,
On markets, shops and dairies;
But the little fellow doesn't want to play:
    Instead he has a yearning
    For unreasonable learning,
    And wants to do Arithmetic all day.
He shows a strong proclivity
For purposeless activity,
And doesn't want experience in clay,
    So I rather think that Roger
    Is a *do*-er, not a dodger,
And how *would* you deal with Roger,
    can you say?

glossary

a flop: failure
proclivity: tendency

unit 2

People and Customs

'An Englishman, even if he lives alone, forms an orderly queue of one.'
George Mikes (1912–1987), Hungarian, lived in England, Critic, broadcaster and writer.

Reading

Lenny Henry was born on 29 August 1958 in the West Midlands of England. His career as a comedian began when, aged 16, he won the talent show *New Faces*. In the seventies he developed his comic impressions on *Tiswas*, an anarchic children's television programme and was then given his own one-man comedy series. He was recently named Showbusiness Personality of the Year. He lives in Berkshire with his wife Dawn French, who is also a comedian.

1 Look at the answers that Lenny Henry gave in a written questionnaire and match them with the questions. Put the correct letter in the boxes provided.

Questionnaire

1 What is your idea of perfect happiness? ☐
2 Which living woman do you most admire? ☐
3 With which historical figure do you most identify? ☐
4 Who would you most like to have been? ☐
5 What is your greatest extravagance? ☐
6 What do you most dislike about your appearance? ☐
7 What was your greatest act of courage? ☐
8 Where would you like to live? ☐
9 What are your favourite names? ☐
10 What is your favourite journey? ☐
11 Who are your favourite musicians? ☐

Lenny Henry's answers

a I buy a lot of records – it's not fair to the shelves, really.

b Steve and Johnny, because they're always the names of heroes in comics and secret-agent films.

c To be totally at peace, in a bath full of chocolate, with a glass of wine and *The Blues Brothers* on television.

d It's a toss-up; on the one hand my wife, Dawn French, who's been an incredible influence on me as a person and as a performer. And also my mum, for coming to Great Britain in the fifties and forging ahead in the face of much adversity.

e Going home.

f Going on stage for the first time.

g Martin Luther King. I've read a lot of his speeches and I admire him for his ability to be articulate and passionate at the same time.

h The size of my bottom when I put on weight.

i Elvis, Digital Underground, The Dust Brothers, Prince, George Clinton, early Stevie Wonder, Van Morrison, Kate Bush, Ry Cooder, Joni Mitchell, Bob Marley, Donald Egan and Ricky Lee Jones (and lots, lots more).

j I like where I'm living now. Eventually when I'm old I'd like to be with my wife by the sea with nice weather.

k Elvis in his travelogue period – he got to kiss more girls than anybody in existence.

Writing

1 Write your own answers to the questionnaire.

1 ....
2 ....
3 ....
4 ....
5 ....
6 ....
7 ....
8 ....
9 ....
10 ....
11 ....

Language Focus

1 Make any corrections necessary to the following sentences.

a I am believing it's a real problem.

b This book is not belonging to me.

c He really annoys me. He continually asks me the same question.

d You're astonishing me.

e I'll come if I can. It's depending on my work.

f Are you knowing my brother?

g He forever telephones me.

h I can't come now. I cook the lunch.

i Do you come with us?

2 Write five sentences using only the words below. You can change the endings if you want to. For example, you can make *tend* into *tendency*.

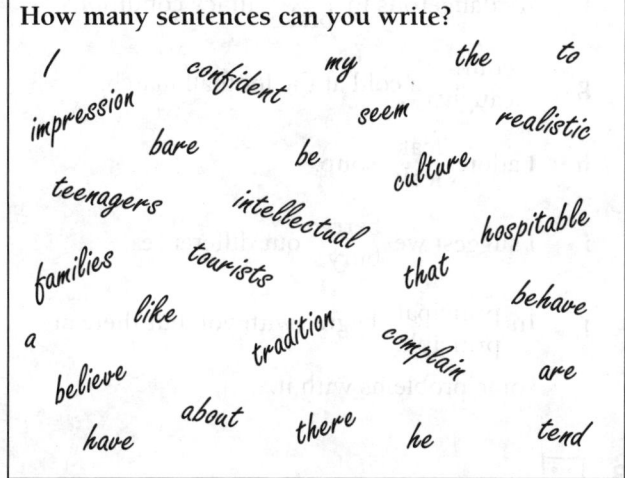

Pronunciation

Homophones are words which are pronounced in the same way but spelt differently.

Example: pair   pear

1 Say the following homophones aloud:

ceiling	sealing	break	brake
weight	wait	court	caught
tyre	tire	leek	leak
tide	tied	bury	berry
sail	sale	principle	principal

2 Circle the correct word in the following sencences.

Example: *I bought a new* pear/(pair) *of shoes.*

a Before the days of sticky tape people used to wrap parcels with sealing/ceiling wax.

b Thank goodness that's over. It's a real wait/weight off my mind.

unit 2

c That's the second burst tyre/tire I've had this month.

d I'm afraid I can't help you. My hands are completely tide/tied.

e There's a huge tear in the sail/sale.

f It's dangerous to break/brake in icy conditions.

g I court/caught a cold at the football match.

h I adore leak/leek soup.

i I suggest we berry/bury our differences.

j In principal/principle I agree with you but there are some problems with it.

3 🔊

Say these tongue-twisters five times each as quickly as you can.

Three thrice-fried thieves.
Deeply dreadful dreams.

4 Complete the box using the clues below.

a not awake
b to have a different opinion
c a group of ships under one command
d an umpire
e a chewy sweet made of boiled sugar and butter
f a plant that climbs up a wall
g to predict or know beforehand
h pleasantly windy
i person who is not present
j an insect with hard shiny wing-covers

ee **sounds**

Vocabulary

1 Label the parts of the tree with these words:

bark   roots   trunk   leaves   twig

2 Look at these statements. If a statement is true, put the letter from column 1 in the square. If it is false, put the letter from column 2 in it. When you have finished read the letters in the squares down. They should spell two words.

	1	2	
All trees have a trunk.	W	A	☐
Affectionate people are cold.	P	E	☐
To come out of your shell means to stop being shy.	L	T	☐
My brother-in-law is the brother of my wife.	L	S	☐
Hospitable people don't invite you to their homes.	I	D	☐
Guy Fawkes tried to blow up the Houses of Parliament.	O	D	☐
An orphan has no mother or father.	N	M	☐
A widower is a woman whose husband has died.	T	E	☐

8

3 An anagram is a word whose letters can be arranged to form a new word. Change the anagrams in the sentences below to form a new word according to the clue given.

Example:

Change **bleat** into a piece of furniture   _table_

a	Change **eat** into a drink.	....
b	Change **night** into an object.	....
c	Change **swell** into places to find water.	....
d	Change **rail** into a teller of lies.	....
e	Change **hose** into footwear.	....
f	Change **heart** into soil.	....
g	Change **slope** into long rounded pieces of wood.	....
h	Change **rare** into the back part.	....
i	Change **tone** into a brief letter.	....
j	Change **doom** into a state of mind.	....

Poem

1 Make as many pairs as possible with the words below.

Example: *a flirtatious smile*

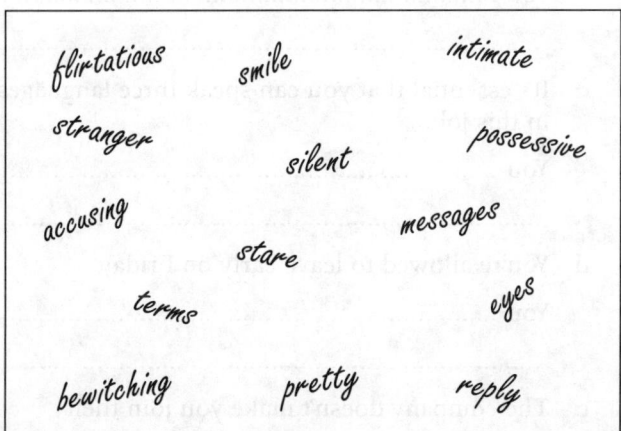

flirtatious, smile, intimate, stranger, silent, possessive, accusing, messages, stare, terms, eyes, bewitching, pretty, reply

2 🔊

Read this poem twice. The first time silently, the second time whispering.

Manwatching   *Georgia Garrett*

From across the party I watch you,
Watching her.
Do my possessive eyes
Imagine your silent messages?
I think not.
She looks across at you
And telegraphs her flirtatious reply.
I have come to recognise this code,
You are on intimate terms with this pretty
    stranger,
And there is nothing I can do.
My face is calm, expressionless,
But my eyes burn into your back
While my insides shout with rage,
She weaves her way towards you,
Turning on a bewitching smile.
I can't see your face, but you are mesmerised I
    expect.
I can predict you; I know this scene so well.
Some acquaintance grabs your arm,
You turn and meet my accusing stare head on,
Her eyes follow yours, meet mine,
And then slide away. She understands,
She's not interested enough to compete.
It's over now.
She fades away, you drift towards me,
'I'm bored' you say, without a trace of guilt,
So we go.
Passing the girl in the hall,
'Bye' I say frostily,
I suppose
You winked.

unit 3

Selling Yourself

'I like work; it fascinates me; I can sit and look at it for hours.'
Jerome K Jerome (1859–1927) English humorous writer and novelist.

Language Focus

1 Read this poem and underline all the lines containing *need* or *have to*.

> **I'd like to be a Teabag** *Peter Dixon*
>
> I'd like to be a teabag,
> And stay at home all day –
> And talk to other teabags
> In a teabag sort of way . . .
>
> I'd love to be a teabag;
> And lie in a little box –
> And never have to wash my face
> Or change my dirty socks . . .
>
> I'd like to be a teabag,
> An Earl Grey one perhaps,
> And doze all day and lie around
> With Earl Grey kind of chaps.
>
> I wouldn't have to do a thing,
> No homework, jobs or chores –
> Comfy in my caddy
> Of teabags and their snores.
>
> I wouldn't have to do exams
> I needn't tidy rooms,
> Or sweep the floor or feed the cat
> Or wash up all the spoons.
>
> I wouldn't have to do a thing,
> A life of bliss – you see . . .
> Except that once in all my life
>
> I'd make a cup of tea!

2 Rewrite all the lines containing *need*. Change *need* to *have to* and start with *He* . . . Rewrite all the lines containing *have to*. Change *have to* to *need* and start with *He* . . .

a ....
....

b ....
....
....

c ....
....

d ....
....
....

e ....
....

3 Rewrite each of the following sentences so that it means the same as the sentence printed above it.

a It isn't necessary to be rich in order to be happy.
   You ....
   ....

b It isn't necessary to have a perfect English accent to get the job.
   You ....
   ....

c It's essential that you can speak three languages in this job.
   You ....
   ....

d You're allowed to leave early on Friday.
   You ....
   ....

e The company doesn't make you join their pension scheme.
   You ....
   ....

f Your boss lets you take time out for training.

You ....

....

g The company makes you have a yearly medical.

You ....

....

h You're allowed to park in the company car park.

You ....

....

i It's important to be loyal to the company at all times.

You ....

....

j You're not supposed to wear jeans.

You ....

....

k In the past you were supposed to always wear a suit.

You ....

....

l Now it isn't necessary to wear a suit.

You ....

....

m You're not allowed to smoke in the office.

You ....

....

n In the past you were allowed to smoke in the office.

You ....

....

o It isn't necessary to clock in.

You ....

....

p In the past the company made you clock in.

You ....

....

4 Fill in the blanks in these sentences using each of the words in the box once.

| most   the least   the worst   much more |
| the least   the more   most of   most of |
| the most   much more   the more |

a .... people retire when they're 60 to 65.

b .... I work ....
.... I want to retire.

c .... my work is dull and routine.

d It's .... boring job I've ever had.

e My boss is by far .... boss I have ever had.

f The job is .... rewarding I have ever had.

g But I'm earning .... money than ever before.

h However, that is .... important thing for me.

i It's just a pity that .... my life is spent working.

j I'd like to be able to spend ....
.... time doing the things I really enjoy.

Reading

1 Read this passage and find words which mean the same as the following:

a a person who lives alone with a simple life style

b faced

c keen, enthusiastic

d making an effort

e a strong desire to do or have something

f an exciting or challenging activity or situation

g to disturb, cause difficulties

h an attempt to achieve something

i unclear or confusing because it can be understood in more than one way

j a shortage

unit 3

On the motivation to work

The hermit sitting in his mountain cell and confronted one day with the Sunday newspaper might be pardoned for wondering why all those people were doing all those things. Why this eager striving to be President of the United States? Why this restless urge to merge, or, with fortunes made, to return again to the fray of business and create yet another empire? Why do all these people buy and sell their houses so ardently, enriching the middlemen, but disrupting families? Why do they change their jobs, divorce their mates, chase the sun or sue their neighbours? Why do they work so hard? Why do they work when they do? Why, come to that, do they work at all?

There must be many pressures and facts which can be called upon to explain any particular set of circumstances. But is there any one set of forces, any general mechanism *within* each of us which pushes us one way or the other? Can we, by looking at the *internal decision process*, answer those questions about work for any given individual or set of individuals? Are people at work dominated by sexuality and aggression, or are they engaged in an endless pursuit of happiness? The body of knowledge about this internal decision process carries the generic title of 'Motivation Theory'.

Motivate is one of those ambiguous words. The dictionary calls it a *transitive* verb. It normally has a subject and an object. X motivates Y, Y is motivated by X. But is X a thing or a person? Can *you* motivate someone? Or is it only money, or hunger, or status, or need for affection? Are you motivated by a lack of something, in the sense that thirst equals lack of liquid, or only by the thing, for example, water? Or is it a mixture? We use the word ambiguously. Does this mean we are unsure of what we really mean by it?

2 People with different orientations tend to choose different jobs to suit their skills and needs.

Match the personalities with the appropriate goals and skills, and with the suitable jobs. Put the correct number or letter in the boxes provided.

Personalities	Goals and skills	Suitable jobs
Realistic		
Social		
Enterprising		
Artistic		
Conventional		
Intellectual		

Goals and skills

a   High energy, enthusiasm, dominance and impulsiveness

b   Interpersonal skills and interest in other people

c   Feelings, intuitions, imagination

d   Objective, concrete goals and tasks, likes to manipulate things – tools, machines, animals, and people

e   Ideas, words and symbols

f   Following the rules and selecting goals approved of by society and customs

Suitable jobs

1   performing arts, writing, painting and music

2   science, teaching or writing

3   social work and counselling and organising others

4   sales, politics, entrepreneurial business or foreign service

5   agriculture, engineering, outdoor conservation work

6   accounting, office work and administration

Writing

Use your notes from **2** to write a short description of each personality.

Example: *Realistic Personality*

Realistic people seek objective, concrete goals and tasks and like to manipulate things – tools, machines, animals, and people. They are best suited to agriculture, engineering, outdoor conservation work and similar practical jobs.

Vocabulary

1 Complete these comparisons with the words from the box below.

| thick thin drunk old sweet tough |
| cunning gentle poor light |

a As .... as a fox.
b As .... as a rake.
c As .... as old boots.
d As .... as pie.
e As .... as a lamb.
f As .... as a feather.
g As .... as two planks.
h As .... as a lord.
i As .... as a churchmouse.
j As .... as the hills.

2

Say the sentences aloud. Remember to use the weak form /əz/ to link the words together.

Example: /./ cunning /əzə/ fox.

3 Fill in the nouns, adverbs and verbs of these adjectives, which can be used to describe people. The last seven do not have a verb form. The first one has been done for you.

Adjective	Noun	Adverb	Verb
sensitive	sensi<u>tiv</u>ity	<u>sen</u>sitively	to sense
assertive	●		
	●		
reliable			
determined			
charming			
adaptable	●		
	●		
authoritative	●		
	●		
creative			
persistent			
weak			
persuasive			
tolerant			
considerate			
patient			
sincere			
enterprising			
honest			
ambitious			
courteous			
loyal			

unit 3

Pronunciation

1 🔲

Underline the stressed syllables on the words you wrote in Vocabulary 3. The first line has been done for you.

Say the words aloud.

2 🔲

Pronounce these *th* words carefully. Decide if the sound is hard (as in *bathe*), or soft (as in *bath*) and put each word in the correct column.

bath   bathe   teeth   teething   birthday
breathe   breath   cloth   clothing   with   south
southern   north   northern   smith   smooth
tenth   faithful   soothe   leather

Hard *th* /ð/ *bathe*   Soft *th* /θ/ *bath*

Can you add more words to either list?

3 Write a tongue-twister using some of the words. Say it five times as quickly as you can.

Poem

1 Match each of these words with its synonym from the list below.

reasonable	....
indifferent	....
to swear (past: swore)	....
stench	....
good breeding	....
rancid	....
booth	....
tar	....
dumbfoundment	....
assent	....

substance for making roads   promise   kiosk
agreement   stale   bad smell   upbringing
not special   fair

2 We sometimes need to 'sell ourselves', for example when trying to get a job. In this poem the speaker is trying to sell himself to a landlady. Read the poem twice. The first time silently, the second time aloud as dramatically as you can.

3 Below are some of the emotions the two speakers might have been feeling during the conversation. Put them in the appropriate column – some may apply to both speakers. Add any of your own that aren't in the list.

angry   embarrassed   impatient   amazed
superior   inferior   nervous   confused
uncomfortable   ashamed

Landlady	Speaker
....	....
....	....
....	....
....	....
....	....
....	....
....	....

Telephone Conversation
Wole Soyinka

The price seemed reasonable, location
Indifferent, The landlady swore she lived
Off premises. Nothing remained
But self-confession. 'Madam,' I warned,
'I hate a wasted journey – I am African.'
Silence. Silenced transmission of
Pressurized good-breeding. Voice, when it came,
Lipstick-coated, long gold-rolled
Cigarette-holder pipped. Caught I was, foully.
'HOW DARK?' . . . I had not misheard. 'ARE YOU LIGHT
OR VERY DARK?' Button B, Button A. Stench
Of rancid breath of public hide-and-speak
Red booth. Red pillar-box. Red double-tiered
Omnibus squelching tar. It *was* real! Shamed
By ill-mannered silence, surrender
Pushed dumbfoundment to beg simplification.
Considerate she was, varying the emphasis –
'ARE YOU DARK? OR VERY LIGHT?' Revelation came.
'You mean – like plain or milk chocolate?'
Her assent was clinical, crushing in its light
Impersonality. Rapidly, wave-length adjusted,
I chose, 'West African sepia' – and as afterthought,
'Down in my passport.' Silence or spectroscopic
Flight of fancy, till truthfulness changed her accent
Hard on the mouthpiece. 'WHAT'S THAT?' conceding
'DON'T KNOW WHAT THAT IS.' 'Like brunette.'
'THAT'S DARK, ISN'T IT?' 'Not altogether.
Facially, I am brunette, but, madam, you should see
The rest of me. Palm of my hand, soles of my feet
Are a peroxide blond, Friction, caused –
Foolishly, madam – by sitting down, has turned
My bottom raven black – One moment, madam!' – sensing
Her receiver rearing on the thunderclap
About my ears – 'Madam,' I pleaded, 'wouldn't you rather
See for yourself?'

glossary
Button B Button A: the buttons in old telephone boxes. Button A to speak, Button B to get your money back.
hide-and-speak: a play on the expression *hide and seek* – a children's game.

unit 4

Memories and Experiences

'The best way to make children is to make them happy.'
Oscar Wilde (1856–1900), British dramatist and poet.

Reading

1

Read and listen to this extract from a novel.

glossary

copper: a large metal container for boiling water
grace: prayer before a meal
beadle: church officer
gruel: thin, watery soup
porriger: measure of food
council: a meeting

Oliver Twist — Charles Dickens

The room in which the boys were fed was a large stone hall, with a copper at one end; out of which the master, dressed in an apron for the purpose, and assisted by one or two women, ladled the gruel at meal-times. Of this festive composition each boy had one porriger, and no more – except on occasions of great public rejoicing, when he had two ounces and a quarter of bread besides. The bowls never wanted washing. The boys polished them with their spoons till they shone again; and when they had performed this operation (which never took very long, the spoons being nearly as large as the bowls), they would sit staring at the copper, with such eager eyes, as if they could have devoured the very bricks of which it was composed; employing themselves, meanwhile, in sucking their fingers most assiduously, with the view of catching up any stray splashes of gruel that might have been cast thereon. Boys have generally excellent appetites. Oliver Twist and his companions suffered the tortures of slow starvation for three months: at last they got so voracious and wild with hunger, that one boy, who was tall for his age, and hadn't been used to that sort of thing (for his father had kept a small cookshop) hinted darkly to his companions that unless he had another basin of gruel *per diem*, he was afraid he might some night happen to eat the boy who slept next him, who happened to be a weakly youth of tender age. He had a wild, hungry eye; and they implicitly believed him. A council was held; lots were cast who should walk up to the master after supper that evening, and ask for more; and it fell to Oliver Twist.

The evening arrived; the boys took their places. The master, in his cook's uniform, stationed himself at the copper; his pauper assistants ranged themselves behind him; the gruel was served out; and a long grace was said over the short commons. The gruel disappeared; the boys whispered to each other, and winked at Oliver; while his next neighbours nudged him. Child as he was, he was desperate with hunger, and reckless with misery. He rose from the table; and advancing to the master, basin and spoon in hand, said, somewhat alarmed at his own temerity:

'Please, sir, I want some more.'

The master was a fat healthy man; but he turned very pale. He gazed in stupefied astonishment on the small rebel for some seconds, and then clung for support to the copper. The assistants were paralysed with wonder; the boys with fear.

'What!' said the master at length, in a faint voice.

'Please, sir,' replied Oliver, 'I want some more.'

The master aimed a blow at Oliver's head with the ladle; pinioned him in his arms; and shrieked aloud for the beadle.

The board were sitting in solemn conclave, when Mr Bumble rushed into the room in great excitement, and addressing the gentleman in the high chair, said, 'Mr Limbkins, I beg your pardon, sir! Oliver Twist has asked for more!'

There was a general start. Horror was depicted on every countenance.

'For *more*!' said Mr Limbkins. 'Compose yourself, Bumble, and answer me distinctly. Do I understand that he asked for more, after he had eaten the supper allotted by the dietary?'

'He did, sir,' replied Bumble.

'That boy will be hung,' said the gentleman in the white waistcoat. 'I know that boy will be hung.'

2 Now read again and find the following words in the passage. Guess the meaning of each one.

to ladle ....
to devour ....
assiduously ....
voracious ....
lots were cast ....
pauper ....
to wink ....
to nudge ....
reckless ....
temerity ....

3 What are the main impressions you get when you read this passage? Underline the words which give you these impressions.

Writing

1 Write a summary of the extract from *Oliver Twist* of not more than thirty words.

2 Read this mini-saga, then expand it into at least three paragraphs.

> **The Shortest Story**
>
> An English Class,
> SIR said, a Short Story
> must contain four principal
> elements, namely,
> RELIGION, SOCIETY, SEX
> and MYSTERY in that order.
> Write story now and
> remember the four elements.
> Five minutes pass,
> boy puts down his pen.
> SIR reads, 'MY GOD said the
> DUCHESS I am PREGNANT,
> WHO DUNNIT!'

Language Focus

1 Fill in the blanks with a suitable form of the verb provided. Remember to use *used to* or *would* (past) where appropriate.

Charles Dickens

Charles Dickens (**a**) .... (born) in 1812 in Portsmouth. The family (**b**) .... (move) to London in 1823. When he was twelve he (**c**) .... (work) in a blacking factory. He worked by a window facing the street and passersby (**d**) .... (pause) and watch him at work. Everyday he (**e**) .... (trudge) through the London streets from Camden Town to Southwark. His family (**f**) .... (be) very poor. His mother (**g**) .... (hope) to open a small school. While she (**h**) .... (try) to do this her husband (**i**) .... (send) to prison for being £40 in debt. When Charles (**j**) .... (be) twenty-four, his first work, *Sketches by Boz*, (**k**) .... (publish). This (**l**) .... (follow) by *Pickwick Papers* with which he (**m**) .... (achieve) financial security and popularity. For the rest of his life work simply (**n**) .... (pour) from his pen. He (**o**) .... (die) of a stroke in 1870.

unit 4

Vocabulary

Animals

1 In this poem the same word is missing in each blank. Read the poem quickly and complete it by adding the word.

Then underline the stressed syllables on the words you wrote in and read the poem aloud.

> **Someone Stole the ....**   *Brian Patten*
>
> While I was taking a short ....-nap
>   someone stole the ....,
> I should have spun round like a ....herine
>   wheel
> When someone stole the ....
> But I was too slow to ....ch them,
>   when someone stole the ....
>
> Now the ....amaran can't float,
>   because someone stole the ....
> And the ....erpillar can't crawl,
>   because someone stole the ....
> And the ....aract can't fall,
>   because someone stole the ....
>
> It was not me and it was not you
>   but it is ....egorically true,
> And if you were to ask me
>   I'd say it was a ....astrophe
>   That someone's stolen the ....

2 The following expressions all include the names of animals. Guess what each one is and write it in. Then match the expressions with their meanings below by putting the correct number in the boxes provided.

a to have a .... in your throat ☐
b to make a .... 's ear of something ☐
c to put the cart before the .... ☐
d to smell a .... ☐
e a .... in a china shop ☐
f till the .... come home ☐
g to let the .... out of the bag ☐
h to put the .... among the
  .... ☐
i to be in the ....-house ☐
j to be a .... in a manger ☐
k information straight from the ....'s mouth ☐
l to cry .... tears ☐
m the black .... of the family ☐
n to keep the .... from the door ☐

1 to refuse to let others have something even though you don't need it yourself
2 a person who has a bad reputation and is disapproved of by their family
3 to reveal a secret when you shouldn't
4 to be able to buy enough food for yourself and family
5 to only pretend to be sad
6 to have doubts and suspicions
7 to not be able to speak properly because your throat is partially blocked
8 information from someone in a position to know that it is true
9 a very long time
10 to do or say something that causes trouble
11 to do things in the wrong order
12 a very clumsy person
13 to be in disgrace
14 to do something very badly

3 Complete the chart below with suitable words.

	Male	Female	Young
a	ram	....	....
b	....	cow	....
c	drake	....	....
d	stallion	....	....
e	....	....	chicken
f	gander	....	gosling
g	....	deer	hind
h	fox	....	....
i	....	lioness	....

18

Pronunciation

1 🔊

Say these tongue-twisters five times each as quickly as you can.

Lame lambs limp.
The horses hard hoofs hit the hard high road.

2 🔊

Choose the words from the box which rhyme with the words below and write them in the second column. The first one has been done for you.

scale   *pail*   ....
site   ....
square   ....
cool   ....
maim   ....
sign   ....
dam   ....
cuff   ....
cow   ....
flew   ....
try   ....
roam   ....
dumb   ....
pain   ....
foul   ....
show   ....

might	drool	through	pail	home	come
bough	owl	high	lamb	frame	prayer
tough	lane	pine	toe		

3 Add one more word that rhymes with each pair.

4 Say the words aloud.

Poem

1 In this poem the rhyming pattern is ababcc. (Lines 1 and 3 rhyme, lines 2 and 4 rhyme, and lines 5 and 6 rhyme). Complete each line with one of the words below. (One pair is spelt the same but not pronounced the same.)

owl blow pail foul owl bowl
snow raw saw wall nail hall

2 Read the poem aloud as atmospherically as you can.

🔊

> **A Winter Song**   William Shakespeare
>
> When icicles hang by the ....,
>   And Dick the shepherd blows his ....,
> And Tom bears logs into the ....,
>   And milk comes frozen home in ....,
> When blood is nipt and ways be ....,
> Then nightly sings the staring ....,
>   Tuwhoo!
> Tuwhit! tuwhoo! A merry note,
> While greasy Joan doth keel the pot.
>
> When all aloud the wind doth ....,
>   And coughing drowns the parson's ....,
> And birds sit brooding in the ....,
>   And Marian's nose looks red and ....,
> When roasted crabs hiss in the ....,
> Then nightly sings the staring ....,
>   Tuwhoo!
> Tuwhit! tuwhoo! A merry note,
> While greasy Joan doth keel the pot.
>
> From *Love's Labour's Lost*

unit 5

Food and Entertainment

'You can always judge a man by what he eats, therefore a country in which there is no free lunch is no longer a free country.'
Arthur Baer, American comic columnist and short-story writer.

Language Focus

1 Fill in the blanks in this recipe with *a*, *an*, *the*, *some*, or leave blank as appropriate.

Cold Caramel Souffles

1

To make (**a**) .... caramel, put (**b**) .... ounces of (**c**) .... sugar with (**d**) .... 4 tablespoons of (**e**) .... water in (**f**) .... small pan over low heat. Cook without stirring until (**g**) .... sugar has dissolved. Increase (**h**) .... heat and boil (**i**) .... syrup rapidly until it is pale golden brown. Remove (**j**) .... pan from (**k**) .... heat and stand it on (**l**) .... cold surface. Add 4 tablespoons of hot water, and pour (**m**) .... caramel into (**n**) .... warm bowl.

2

Dissolve (**a**) .... gelatine in (**b**) .... 3 tablespoons of (**c**) .... warm water to which (**d**) .... lemon juice had been added. Separate (**e**) .... eggs and beat (**f**) .... 3 egg yolks with (**g**) .... 2 tablespoons of (**h**) .... caster sugar in (**i**) .... bowl. Place (**j**) .... bowl over (**k**) .... pan of (**l**) .... hot water and beat (**m**) .... egg mixture until it thickens. Remove (**n**) .... bowl and let (**o**) .... egg mixture cool. Blend (**p**) .... caramel and (**q**) .... dissolved gelatine thoroughly into (**r**) .... egg mixture. Leave to cool.

3

Whisk (**a**) .... 2 egg whites until stiff, and lightly whisk (**b**) .... cream. When (**c**) .... souffle mixture is cold, but not completely set, fold in (**d**) .... cream and (**e**) .... egg whites. Spoon (**f**) .... mixture into individual souffle dishes to set. Chill for about 30 minutes.

2 Write out in full the instructions below (they are in the right order). Use some of the following words to link the sentences together.

next first then finally at the same time lastly

Make the caramel
Dissolve the gelatine
Separate the eggs
Place the bowl over a pan of hot water
Whisk the egg whites
Fold in the cream and egg whites
Spoon the mixture into individual souffle dishes and chill

....
....
....
....
....
....
....
....
....

3 Expand each of these headlines into a sentence to describe what the article is about. Use a relative clause in your sentence. The first one has been done for you.

a 50 HURT IN BOMB EXPLOSION
This article is about...... *a bomb explosion which hurt 50 people.*

b PICASSO SOLD £100,000
This article is about................................
....

c   INTEREST RATES INCREASED 1%

This article tells us about ....
....

d   15 PROTESTERS IMPRISONED

This story is about..............................
....

e   PLANE HIJACKED KENYA

This article is about..............................
....

f   ROADS N.W. SCOTLAND FLOODED

This is a warning about..............................
....

g   SHARE PRICES RISEN DRAMATICALLY

This article tells us about..............................
....

h   HURRICANE DAMAGED NATIONAL GALLERY

This story is about..............................
....

i   HUMAN TEMPLE DISCOVERED KENT

This article is about..............................
....

j   OVERTURNED LORRY BLOCKED M25

This is a warning about..............................
....

Pronunciation

1 These foods are typical British combinations. Complete each pair using the words below.

lemon   onions   sugar   butter
biscuits   bacon   chips

fish and ....   beef and ....
bread and ....   cheese and ....
eggs and ....   ice and ....
milk and ....

Say the phrases aloud using the weak form /ən/ and linking the words together.

Example: *tea /ən/ biscuits*

2 Say the words of the song as rhythmically as possible. The stressed words are underlined for you.

King Caractacus

The <u>la</u>dies of the <u>ha</u>rem of the <u>court</u> of King Ca<u>rac</u>tacus,
Were <u>just</u> <u>pass</u>ing <u>by</u>.

The <u>no</u>ses on the <u>fa</u>ces of
the <u>la</u>dies of the <u>ha</u>rem of the <u>court</u> of King Ca<u>rac</u>tacus,
Were <u>just</u> <u>pass</u>ing <u>by</u>.

The <u>boys</u> who put the <u>pow</u>der on
the <u>no</u>ses on the <u>fa</u>ces of
the <u>la</u>dies of the <u>ha</u>rem of the <u>court</u> of King Ca<u>rac</u>tacus,
Were <u>just</u> <u>pass</u>ing <u>by</u>.

The <u>fas</u>cinating <u>wit</u>ches who put the <u>scin</u>tillating <u>sti</u>tches in the <u>bree</u>ches of
the <u>boys</u> who put the <u>pow</u>der on
the <u>no</u>ses on the <u>fa</u>ces of
the <u>la</u>dies of the <u>ha</u>rem of the <u>court</u> of King Ca<u>rac</u>tacus,
Were <u>just</u> <u>pass</u>ing <u>by</u>.

If you <u>want</u> to take some <u>pic</u>tures of
the <u>fas</u>cinating <u>wit</u>ches who put the <u>scin</u>tillating <u>sti</u>tches in the <u>bree</u>ches of
the <u>boys</u> who put the <u>pow</u>der on
the <u>no</u>ses on the <u>fa</u>ces of
the <u>la</u>dies of the <u>ha</u>rem of the court of King Ca<u>rac</u>tacus.

<u>You're</u> <u>too</u> <u>late</u>!
Because they've <u>just</u> <u>passed</u> <u>by</u>!

unit 5

Vocabulary

1 Fill in the blanks with suitable words.

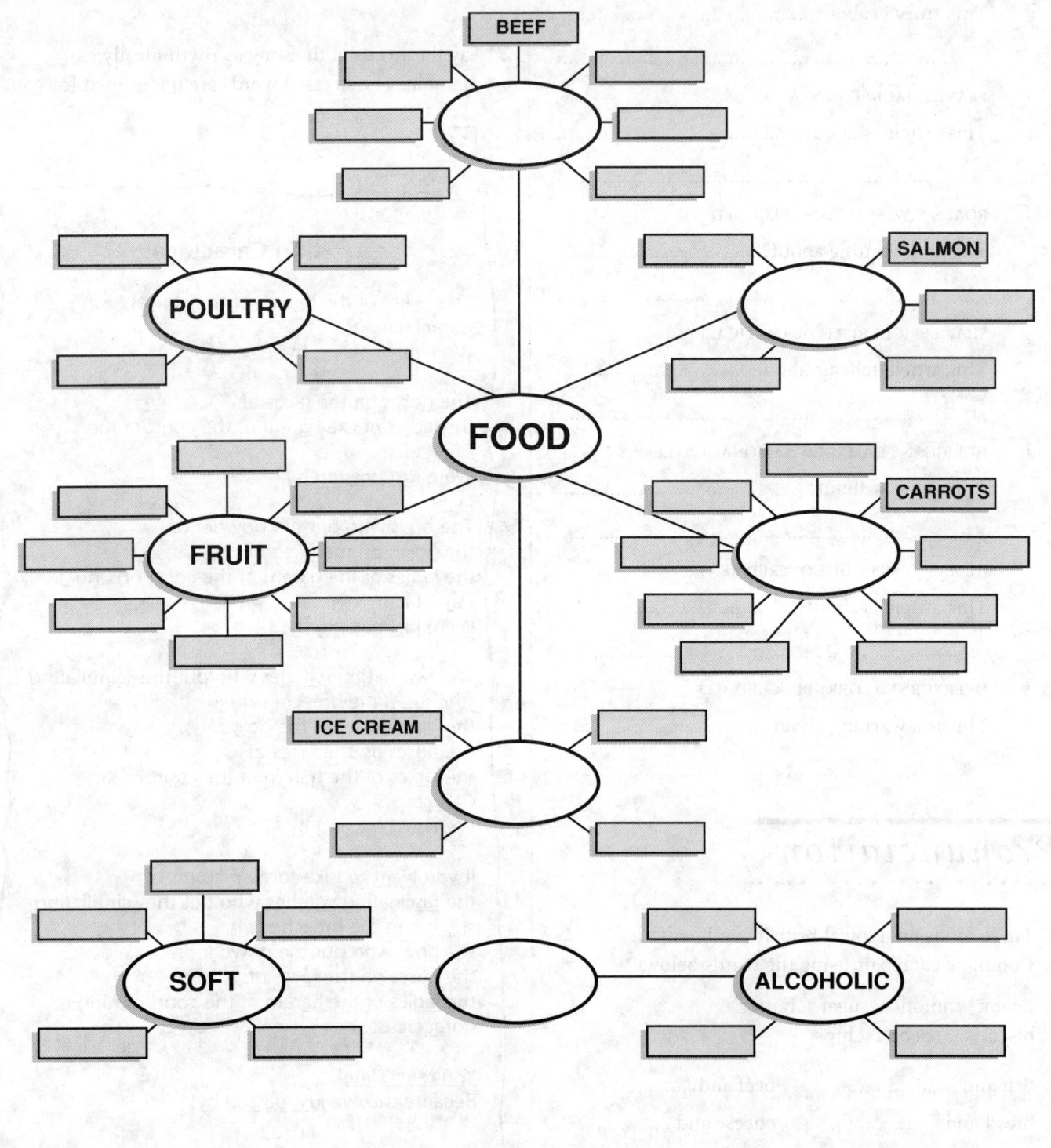

2 Complete these sentences with an adjective plus a noun. The first one has been done for you.

a If you crush peppercorns you get
   crushed peppercorns

b If you marinate meat you get
   ....

c If you chop onions you get
   ....

d If you dice carrots you get
   ....

e If you mull wine you get
   ....

f If you mash potatoes you get
   ....

g If you slice bread you get
   ....

h If you boil water you get
   ....

i If you grind coffee you get
   ....

j If you bake potatoes you get
   ....

k If you sift flour you get
   ....

l If you grate a lemon you get
   ....

Reading

1 *West End Theatre Guide*

Look at these newspaper adverts for what's on at the theatres. They don't all give the same amount of information. Ask questions to find the missing information.

OUT OF ORDER
Shaftesbury WC2. 379 5399 Mon – Fri 8.00–10.00 Sat 8.30 (£5.50–16.50)

ABSURD PERSON SINGULAR
Aykbourn's wonderfully dark production of his 1970s comedy about three middle-class couples. Whitehall SW1 968 1119. Mon – Sat (£9.50–15.50)

THE PHANTOM OF THE OPERA
Her Majesty's SW1. Mon – Sat 7.45 – 10.20 (£8.50–25.00)

BLOOD BROTHERS
Willy Russell's grand, tear-jerking musical. Twin brothers are separated at birth – do their characters or their upbringings affect their fate? Albery WC2. 867 1115 Mon – Sat. 7.45–10.45.

SHIRLEY VALENTINE
Elizabeth Estensen in Willy Russell's successful comedy. Duke of York's WC2. 836 5122 (£6.50–15.50)

PRIVATE LIVES
Coward's brittle comedy with Keith Baxter and Joan Collins.
Mon – Fri 8.00 – 10.20, Sat. 8.30 (£8 – 18.50)

unit 5

Writing

1 Choose a play or film or concert you have been to recently and write a review of it for your local newspaper. Briefly describe the content, and comment on the performance.

Poem

1 Imagine you are the following fruit and vegetables. Complete the sentences. Try to think of a different answer for each sentence.

a a carrot:
"I don't like it when people .... "

b a peach:
"I don't like it when people .... "

c an orange:
"I don't like it when people .... "

d a tomato:
"I don't like it when people .... "

e a potato:
"I don't like it when people .... "

f a pea:
"I don't like it when people .... "

g a sprout:
"I don't like it when people .... "

h a cabbage:
"I don't like it when people .... "

i an onion:
"I don't like it when people .... "

2 Read the poem twice. The first time silently, the second time aloud.

Vegetarians *Roger McGough*

Vegetarians are cruel, unthinking people.
Everybody knows that a carrot screams when grated.
That a peach bleeds when torn apart.
Do you believe an orange insensitive
to thumbs gouging out its flesh?
That tomatoes spill their brains painlessly?
Potatoes, skinned alive and boiled,
the soil's little lobsters.
Don't tell me it doesn't hurt
when peas are ripped from the scrotum,
the hide flayed off sprouts,
cabbage shredded, onions beheaded,

Throw in the trowel
and lay down the hoe.
Mow no more
Let my people go!

Legal and Illegal

'If the laws could speak for themselves, they would complain of the lawyers in the first place.'
George Savile Halifax (1633–1695), English Statesman and essayist.

Vocabulary

1 Who are these people?

Complete the box using the clues below.

a someone who breaks into a house to steal
b someone who makes false notes or coins
c a person who deliberately kills another
d a person pretending to be what s/he is not
e someone who imports goods without paying tax
f someone who takes someone away by force, usually in order to demand money
g someone who threatens to do something unpleasant to someone unless they give them money
h someone who takes control of a vehicle by force to make it travel to a different place
i someone who uses violence, for example bombing, for political reasons to force a government to do something

2 Prefixes *in-*, *dis-*, *un-*, *im-*, *il-*
Complete each sentence with the appropriate adjective from the lists below.

il-	*un-*	*dis-*
illegal	unfair	disbelieve
illegitimate	untruthful	dishonest
illiterate	unbiased	disloyal
illogical	unidentified	disobey

im-	*in-*
immoral	invalid
immature	incredible
impartial	independent
impolite	inaccurate

a The evidence of the defendant's wife was .... because it was neither .... nor ....
b I .... everything he said because he is so .... and ....
c It's difficult to give evidence against a friend because it makes you feel so ....
d The witness couldn't read the statement because he was ....
e I couldn't understand his argument. It was so ....
f The police have not released the name of the victim as the body is still ....
g The Duke's daughter couldn't inherit his estate because she was ....
h He is an .... witness, but it's difficult to take him seriously as he is so ....
i Forgery is ....
j He was punished for a crime he didn't commit which is very ....
k He said I .... him which is totally ....
l It's .... to give false evidence.
m I'm amazed he won the case. It's quite ....
n He lost all my support when he was so .... to the witness.

unit 6

3 Add one of the prefixes *dis-, un-, in-, im-* to the pairs of words below to form their opposites.

a ....comprehensible ....direct
b ....comfortable ....reliable
c ....advantage ....interested
f ....probable ....mobile

4 Put each word from the list with the correct prefix below to form its opposite.

predictable pure employed connect
satisfaction moderate significant personal
sincere conscious integrate correct

dis.................... un....................
dis.................... un....................
dis.................... un....................
in.................... im....................
in.................... im....................
in.................... im....................

5 Add a prefix to each of the following words to give their opposite meaning.

a ....do f ....dress
b ....sufficient g ....content
c ....operative h ....acceptable
d ....satisfactory i ....equality
e ....educated j ....appropriate

Writing

1 Complete this dialogue between a Defendant (D) and a Prosecutor (P) in a court trial.

P: Are you Martin Benson of Oaten Hill Place, Newcastle?

D: ....

P: Okay. Now, will you please tell the court where you were on the afternoon of January 31 1981?

D: ....

P: Who did you go to the football match with?

D: ....

P: And what's your brother's name?

D: ....

P: Is that John with an 'h' or without an 'h'?

D: ....

P: With. Why did you go to this match in Cardiff? It's a long way from Newcastle.

D: ....

P: What's he studying there?

D: ....

P: Did you say 'tourism', or 'terrorism'?

D: ....

P: I think that you said 'terrorism'. That is a very interesting 'slip of the tongue'.

2 When we write a conversation there are many verbs we can use instead of *said* which can indicate the content of the conversation, the way the words were said or the mood of the speaker. Write what you think these people said.

Example: *'Okay, I'll do it'*, he agreed.

a ………………………………………he threatened.
b ………………………………………she advised.
c ………………………………………she warned.
d ………………………………………she sobbed.
e ………………………………………he moaned.
f ………………………………………she sighed.
g ………………………………………he laughed.
h ………………………………………she shouted.
i ………………………………………he whispered.
j ………………………………………he snapped.

Language Focus

1 Write out in reported speech the dialogue you completed in Writing 1.

2 Change into reported speech the sentences you wrote in Writing 2. For a, b and c use the verbs provided. For the others use *say* or *tell*.

a ……………………………………………
b ……………………………………………
c ……………………………………………
d ……………………………………………
e ……………………………………………
f ……………………………………………
g ……………………………………………

h ……………………………………………
i ……………………………………………
j ……………………………………………

Reading

From the Files of Inspector Craig

Inspector Leslie Craig of Scotland Yard has kindly consented to release some of his case histories for the benefit of those interested in the application of logic to the solution of crimes.

1 Read *The Case of the Identical Twins* and write your answer below.

The Case of the Identical Twins

In this interesting case, a robbery occurred in London. Three well-known criminals **A**, **B** and **C** were rounded up for questioning. Now, **A** and **C** happened to be identical twins and few people could tell them apart. All three suspects had elaborate records, and a good deal was known about their personalities and habits. In particular, the twins were quite timid, and neither one ever dared to pull a job without an accomplice. **B**, on the other hand, was quite bold and despised ever using an accomplice. Also several witnesses testified that at the time of the robbery, one of the two twins was seen drinking at a bar in Dover, but it was not known which twin. Again, assuming that no-one other than **A**, **B** or **C** was involved in the robbery, which ones are innocent and which ones guilty?

………………… must be guilty
……………………………………………
……………………………………………
……………………………………………
……………………………………………

………………… can't be guilty
……………………………………………
……………………………………………
……………………………………………
……………………………………………

unit 6

2 Case of the Four

This time four suspects **A**, **B**, **C** and **D** were rounded up for questioning concerning a robbery. It was known for sure that at least one of them was guilty and that no-one outside these four was involved. The following facts turned up:

a   A was definitely innocent.
b   If **B** was guilty, then s/he had exactly one accomplice.
c   If **C** was guilty, then s/he had exactly two accomplices.

Inspector Craig was especially interested in knowing whether **D** was innocent or guilty, since **D** was a particularly dangerous criminal. Fortunately, the above facts are sufficient to determine this.

Is D guilty or not? Write your answer and explanation below.

....
....
....
....
....

Pronunciation

1 [cassette]

The following words are often said without one of the syllables.
Cross out the 'lost' syllable in the following words.

Example: illit*e*rate

vegetable   terrific   considerate   comfortable
stationery   murderer   different   vocabulary
scandalous   several   explanatory   monastery
business   literary   desperate   prosperous
interesting   dictionary   originally   naturally

2 *Odd one out*

Say these words aloud and circle the word that has a different vowel sound. Then add one or two more to the list that sound the same as the words you didn't circle.

a   define   remind   apologise   definite   contrite
    ....

b   enough   rough   cough   tough   stuff
    ....

c   bear   dear   mayor   stare   fair
    ....

d   fear   ear   steer   deer   pear
    ....

Poem

1 This poem has rhyming couplets. (Each pair of lines rhymes.) Fill in the gaps with an appropriate word from the list below.

stare   thin   spare   depravity   square   stifled
there   awake   uncombed   stair   suavity
thumbs   away   way   known   repair   law
Crime   cards   gravity   air

2 The poem has a very regular beat of four beats to each line. Underline the four syllables in each line that are on the beat. The first verse has been done for you.

Now read the poem aloud.

Macavity the Mystery Cat   T S Eliot

Macavity's a Mystery Cat: he's called the Hidden Paw –
For he's the master criminal who can defy the ....
He's the bafflement of Scotland Yard, the Flying Squad's despair:
For when they reach the scene of crime – *Macavity's not ....!*

Macavity, Macavity, there's no-one like Macavity,
He's broken every law, he breaks the law of ....
His powers of levitation would make a fakir ....
And when you reach the scene of crime – *Macavity's not there!*
You may see him in the basement, you may look up in the .... –
But I tell you once and once again, *Macavity's not there!*

Macavity's a ginger cat, he's very tall and ....;
You would know him if you saw him, for his eyes are sunken in,
His brow is deeply lined with thought, his head is highly domed;
His coat is dusty from neglect, his whiskers are ....
He sways his head from side to side, with movement like a snake;
And when you think he's half asleep, he's always wide ....

Macavity, Macavity, there's no-one like Macavity,
For he's a fiend in feline shape, a monster of ....
You may meet him in a by-street, you may see him in the .... –
But when a crime's discovered, then *Macavity's not there!*

He's outwardly respectable. (They say he cheats at ....)
And his footprints are not found in any file of Scotland Yard's.
And when the larder's looted, or the jewel-case is rifled,
Or when the milk is missing, or another peke's been .... ,
Or the greenhouse glass is broken, and the trellis past .... –
Ay, there's the wonder of the thing! *Macavity's not there!*

And when the Foreign Office find a Treaty's gone astray.
Or the Admiralty lose some plans and drawings by the .... ,
There may be a scrap of paper in the hall or on the .... –
But it's useless to investigate – *Macavity's not there!*
And when the loss has been disclosed, the Secret Service say,
"It *must* have been Macavity!" – but he's a mile ....
You'll be sure to find him resting, or a-licking of his .... ,
Or engaged in doing complicated long division sums.

Macavity, Macavity, there's no-one like Macavity,
There never was a Cat of such deceitfulness and ....
He always has an alibi, and one or two to ....:
At whatever time the deed took place – MACAVITY WASN'T THERE!
And they say that all the Cats whose wicked deeds are widely ....
(I might mention Mungojerrie, I might mention Griddlebone)
Are nothing more than agents for the Cat who all the time
Just controls their operations: The Napoleon of ....!

glossary

bafflement: perplexity
Scotland Yard: the Headquarters of the Metropolitan (London) Police Force
fakir: a religious poor man, or 'magic' man
Peke: short for pekinese = a kind of dog

unit 7

Our Surroundings

'Why did Nature create man? Was it to show that she is big enough to make mistakes, or was it pure ignorance?'
Holbrook Jackson (1847–1948), English journalist, editor, and author.

Reading

Mother Nature Awards

One of the biggest modern industries is the manufacture of awards, whether it's rosettes for restaurants, Oscars for films, or prizes for books. The strange thing is, though, that all these prizes are for man-made things. Natural things never get a look in. Here, Miles Kington introduces the idea of awarding prizes of his own to things in nature which deserve them.

1 Match the winners to the descriptions below. Put the appropriate number in each box.

a Special Design Award for being Useless Yet Much in Demand
– GRASS ☐
b For Outstanding Design and Downright Terrible Public Relations Image
– THE IVY ☐
c Least Useful Four-legged Animal Award
– THE LLAMA ☐
d Special Award for Adaptability
– THE SEAGULL ☐
e Species Most Deserving Extinction
– THE PANDA ☐
f Prize for Outstanding Use of P. R. (Public Relations)
– THE ROBIN ☐

1 I'm sorry, but it's true. All right, so it has this cuddly image, but the reality is quite different. It's big and surly, and it has the madness to like eating a certain sort of bamboo which is not only difficult to find but upsets its stomach. Its habitat has almost vanished. It seems unable to work out how to have children successfully, and it doesn't do anything, just sits around all day waiting for people to come and go 'Ooooh, isn't it lovely.' No it's not. We waste so much time and money on this layabout, which could be spent on something much more deserving.

2 This is as good a climber in its own way as bindweed – better, perhaps, considering its little suckers – but it also has outstandingly bad image problems. People are convinced that it kills trees, plants, buildings, etc, so it gets destroyed a lot. There is absolutely no need for this as, if anything, it helps to keep things up. Perhaps it is the poisonous berries which help to give it a bad name; this aspect could be redesigned in future. Other species which have good design and bad image trouble are spiders and cockroaches.

3 I did consider giving this to the fox, actually, which has successfully made the transition from a country animal, where it is hunted, to being a town animal, where it is cosseted. But this bird has made such a magnificent transition from being a seaside animal, where it was forced to hunt for fish all day, to being a ravager of city rubbish dumps, where everything is provided for it free, that I felt it deserved the top award.

4 Well-known to naturalists as one of the greediest, most violent, most jealous and even murderous of birds (the alligator of the bird world), nevertheless it has easily maintained an image of being friendly and approachable by pretending a friendship with people, perching on their forks while they are digging, etc, singing a most merry little song which loosely translated means: 'this is my territory and I will kill all invaders'. Getting on to Christmas cards was its master stroke.

5 This is not, of course, useless, as farm animals eat it, but statistics show that most of it is cut and then thrown away, as if it were useless. Do you ever keep it? Well then. It has also developed the knack of being cut constantly and growing again, as if it liked it, whereas most otherwise tough plants hate being mown. It is the only plant which we prize most when it is only an inch high, and which we walk on to show we like it.

6 What defeated the Incas was having this less-than-useless animal. It cannot carry a person, either into or out of battle. It will not give much milk. Its hair is too coarse to be pleasant, and the same goes for its meat. Into the bargain, it is bad-tempered and it spits.

2 Find the following words in the text and give a synonym or definition

a surly..
b suckers...
c to cosset..
d a ravager...
e to perch...
f a knack..
g to mow..
h coarse...

Language Focus

1 Combine these sentences with *if*. You may have to make them negative and change some of the words.

a We spend a lot of time and money on the panda. We could spend it on something more deserving.

If ....

....

b Ivy has poisonous berries. This gives it a bad name.

If ....

....

c Ivy has bad image problems. People destroy it.

If ....

....

d The seagull is very adaptable. It won the special award for adaptability.

If ....

....

e The robin pretends to be friendly and approachable. It is often on Christmas cards.

If ....

....

f The llama cannot carry a person or give much milk. It won the Least Useful Four-legged Animal Award.

If ....

....

2 Rewrite these sentences replacing *if* with the word in brackets.

a House prices won't rise if interest rates stay so high. (unless)

....

b The house market will stay dead if the inflation rate doesn't fall. (as long as)

....

c I'll buy your house if I can sell mine. (provided that)

....

d I'll buy your house if I can move in next month. (on condition that)

....

e I would have bought your house if the surveyor hadn't advised me against it. (but for the fact that)

....

f If I bought your house then I could walk to work every day. (supposing)

....

Vocabulary

1 Match the people in box A to the places they live in in box B.

A	monk eskimo gypsy queen soldier camper a rich person a very poor person artist

B	slum tent palace monastery studio barracks caravan igloo mansion

2 Match the animals in column to the places they live in in box B.

A	rabbit budgerigar cow horse pig dog fish

B	kennel aquarium sty cage stable shed hutch

unit 7

3 Here are the meanings of ten verbs all meaning *to go*, but in different ways. Complete the box by matching the correct verb to its meaning.

a to run very quickly for a short distance
b to walk smartly in step, as in the army
c to walk in a leisurely way
d to walk as if lame
e to walk like a duck
f to walk slowly wasting time
g to walk fast with long steps
h to move with short tottering steps, like a baby
i to walk in a stiff, self-important way
j to move in a lazy, tired way

waddle sprint dawdle limp strut
toddle march stroll slouch stride

4 Put these words on the staircase in order of speed.

run dash walk wander hobble
stroll dawdle saunter sprint rush

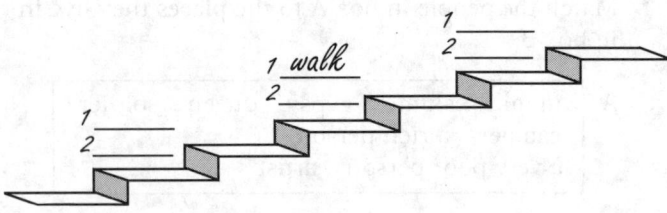

5 Circle the odd one out:

a jumped leapt bounded crawled
b marched strode strolled strutted
c limped rushed hobbled tottered
d soared swooped dived pounced
e fluttered paced flitted frisked
f strolled dawdled strode sauntered

Writing

1 Write a short scenario about one of the following. Use some of the interesting verbs and adjectives that you have learned in this unit.

a *Characters*: a giant, a baby, an old woman
   Place: a cottage in a forest
   Plot: the giant tries to kidnap the baby
          the old lady makes a deal with him

b *Characters*: an actor, an actress, a director
   Place: a theatre
   Plot: the actress refuses to be in a play with the actor
          the director makes a deal with her

c *Characters*: a bank manager, a bank robber, a cashier
   Place: a bank
   Plot: the robber tries to rob the bank

Pronunciation

1

Say these limericks aloud. Link the words together where marked and stress the syllables.

There was a young man of Bengal,
Who went to a fancy dress ball,
He thought he would risk it,
And go as a biscuit,
But a dog ate him up in the hall.

There was a young lady from Riger,
Who went for a ride on a tiger,
They returned from the ride
With the lady inside
And a smile on the face of the tiger.

2

If you say each of these author's names linked together it sounds like other words. Match each author to the correct book and write the name out in words. The first one has been done for you.

Chris P Bacon   Eva Brick   Rhoda Camel
Eileen Doubt   Watts E Dunn   Gladys Friday
Wendy Go   Lee King   Arthur Letic   S. K. Mow
Anna Rack   Vic Tree   Walter Wall

Poem

1 Read the poem twice. The first time silently, the second time aloud.

2 Either: Draw a picture of the poem.
   Or: Write a short description of his birthplace.

I Remember, I Remember
Thomas Hood

I remember, I remember,
The house where I was born,
The little window where the sun
Came peeping in at morn;
He never came a wink too soon,
Nor brought too long a day,
But now, I often wish the night
Had borne my breath away!

I remember, I remember,
The roses, red and white,
The violets, and the lily-cups,
Those lovers made of light!
The lilacs where the robin built,
And where my brother set
The laburnum on his birthday, –
The tree is living yet!

I remember, I remember,
Where I was used to swing,
And thought the air must rush as fresh
To swallows on the wing;
My spirit flew in feathers then,
That is so heavy now,
And summer pools could hardly cool
The fever on my brow!

I remember, I remember,
The fir trees dark and high;
I used to think their slender tops
Were close against the sky:
It was a childish ignorance,
But now 'tis little joy
To know I'm farther off from heaven
Than when I was a boy.

unit 8

Education

'I have never let school interfere with my education.'
Mark Twain (1835 – 1910), American humorous writer and wit.

Vocabulary

1 Circle the correct spelling of the words below.

   Example: ~~necessary~~   neccessary

   a   friend   freind
   b   appearance   appearence
   c   recieve   receive
   d   hight   height
   e   begining   beginning
   f   developing   developping
   g   notable   noteable
   h   arguement   argument
   i   attach   attatch
   j   address   adress
   k   foreign   foriegn

2 Write the nouns from these verbs. They all end with *-ion*.

   Example: negotiate   *negotiation*

   a   explore   ....
   b   classify   ....
   c   deceive   ....
   d   subscribe   ....
   e   hesitate   ....
   f   oppose   ....
   g   repeat   ....
   h   specify   ....
   i   combine   ....
   j   cancel   ....
   k   contribute ....
   l   alter   ....
   m   inform   ....
   n   suspect   ....
   o   explain   ....

Pronunciation

1 🔊

Underline the stressed syllables on the words in Vocabulary 2, and say the words aloud.

2 🔊

Silent Letters
Some words contain 'silent' letters that aren't pronounced. Cross out the silent consonant(s) in the following words.

Example: answ~~e~~r

a   listen   n   half
b   whistle   o   could
c   lamb   p   walk
d   debt   q   Wednesday
e   autumn   r   handkerchief
f   psychology   s   cupboard
g   whole   t   Christmas
h   write   u   foreign
i   right   v   knee
j   knock   w   plumber
k   palm   x   sign
l   daughter   y   yacht
m   honest   z   character

Now say the words aloud.

Reading

1 Read the poem once and then fill in each of the blanks with a suitable preposition.

Spell it *Mike Rosen*

1. We didn't used (**a**) .... have
POETRY
(**b**) .... our class
we used (**c**) .... have
SPELLING
instead,
Each week, every Friday,
the teacher used (**d**) .... write (**e**) .... 12 words
(**f**) .... the blackboard
and she'd say
LEARN THEM!
Then we had (**g**) .... write them (**h**) ....
(**i**) .... our notebooks.

2. You didn't have (**a**) .... know that the words meant,
You didn't even have to know how (**b**) .... say them.
All you had (**c**) .... know was how to spell them.

3. There was the word
SEPULCHRE
I was always sure it was said
SEEP_ULL_KREE.
I still don't know what a sepulchre is.
So come the next Friday
she rubbed all the words (**a**) .... the board
and she goes;
YOU!
(pointing (**b**) .... you)
HOW DO YOU SPELL
SEPULCHRE?
And you sat there going
errr . . . errr . . .
WHAT'S IT BEGIN (**c**) ...., FOOL?
err . . . s?
THEN?
err . . .i?
NO FOOL.
YOU BOY, WHAT COMES NEXT?
I don't know.
WHAT? BUT YOU'VE
HAD A WHOLE WEEK
(**d**) .... LEARN IT.
I had to see the doctors, miss,
EVERY NIGHT?
No miss.

4. You just felt terrible.
Each week, every Friday,
you sat there.
Woud the finger be pointing (**a**) .... you?

5. Friday morning
(**a**) .... the way to school
A, S, P, err
(quick glance (**b**) .... the notebook)
A, R, er
(quick glance (**c**) .... the notebook)
A no I mean U, U?
(quick glance (**d**) .... notebook)
yes U
S
ASPARAGUS
into school
The finger.
YOU BOY
Oh no . . .
here we go again.

6. Then she gave us
DICTIONARIES . . . wow.
and once
me and Harrybo
we were going (**a**) .... it (**b**) .... rude words.

7. But they weren't there.
I mean it was
'NELSON'S FIRST DICTIONARY'.
Dark blue cover.
And it just didn't have the words (**a**) ....
none (**b**) .... them.
So there we were giggling (**c**) ....
a word that was (**d**) ....
that wasn't rude
but if you read it another way
it could be rude . . .
And she saw us
and she goes,
I HOPE YOU TWO ARE NOT LOOKING (**e**) ....
SOMETHING INDECENT.
No, miss,
says Harrybo,
we're laughing
(**f**) .... an old joke.
GOOD,
she says, glaring.
She was dead good (**g**) .... glaring

8. And I was thinking she's going to come (**a**) ....
and look (**b**) .... the page
and find (**c**) ....
and it will be a rude word
and we'll really get it.

9. I glanced (**a**) .... at the page
and I saw
KISS
so I thought
if she asks, what word?
I'll say, we were looking (**b**) .... KISS
(because that's sort (**c**) .... nearly rude, isn't it?)
But she believed Harrybo's story (**d**) .... the old joke,
GOOD
she says
and went (**e**) ....
still GLARING.

10. I think she thought words are OK
so long (**a**) .... all you do is spell them.
What starts getting really messy
is when people find (**b**) ....
what words mean . . .

Language Focus

1 Complete these sentences with suitable endings. Include a verb in each of your endings after choosing the correct preposition.

a I'm quite fond ....

b Your promotion depends ....

c He was accused ....

d It's difficult to choose ....

e My job consists ....

f I've always been interested ....

g She's decided ....

h I'm fed up ....

i He was found guilty ....

j I'm responsible ....

k I'm determined ....

l He's involved ....

m I forgot ....

n It's very hard to stop ....

o Do you remember ....

p She succeeded ....

2 Circle the best linking words in the following passage.

When I was at school I always hated Fridays because that was the day we had to get to school early and (a) *moreover / on the other hand / however* we had our spelling test. If we got less than 90% right we had to stay in after school and do the text again. (b) *Furthermore / Whereas / Therefore* we got a 'black star' and if you had three 'black stars' you had to go to the headmaster. I was hopeless at spelling (c) *whereas / however / although* my best friend was really good at it. (d) *Moreover / On the other hand / As* I was really good at arithmetic tables (e) *therefore / whilst / what's more* my friend could never remember them. So whenever we could, we told each other the answers.

Writing

1 Think back to your early school days and write a short account of something that you didn't or did like doing.

Poem

1 You're going to read a poem about a gossip, a 'nosey-parker', a 'busy-body'. Try to guess the answers to these questions before reading the poem.

   a What does she say the girl at Number Three has given her boy-friend?

      ....
....

   b What does she say the woman in the upstairs flat has bought?

      ....
....

   c What does her daughter say about 'gossip'?

      ....
....

   d What does she say Mr Thompson is doing?

      ....
....

   e What is her daughter studying?

      ....
....

2 Now read the poem and write in its answers to the questions above.

   a ....
....

   b ....
....

   c ....
....

   d ....
....

   e ....
....

The Proper Study   W S Slater

Seated before her window Mrs Jones
Described the passers-by in ringing tones.
'Look', she would say, 'the girl at Number Three
Has brought her latest boy-friend home to tea;
And, see, the woman at the upstairs flat
Has bought herself another summer hat.'
Her daughter Daphne, filled with deep disgust,
Expostulated 'Mother, really must
You pry upon the neighbours? Don't you know
Gossip is idle, empty-minded, low?'
And Mrs Jones would murmur 'Fancy, dear!
There's Mr Thompson going for his beer.'

Daphne, an earnest girl of twenty-three,
Read Sociology for her degree
And every Saturday she would repair,
Armed with her tutor's latest questionnaire,
To knock on doors, demanding 'are you wed?
Have you a child? A car? A double bed?'
Poor Mrs Jones would remonstrate each week,
'Daphne, I wonder how you have the cheek.
And then to call me nosey!' Daphne sighed.
'Oh, will you never understand?' she cried.
'Mere curiosity is one thing, Mother:
Social Analysis is quite another.'

glossary

expostulate: to argue
repair (here): to go
remonstrate: to protest
the cheek (here): impudence

unit 9

How it works

'England and America are two countries separated by the same language.'
Oscar Wilde (1856 – 1900), British dramatist, poet and wit.

Reading

How to climb through a playing card.
How to fold a napkin into a fan.

1 Look at these pictures and decide which of the two processes they illustrate.

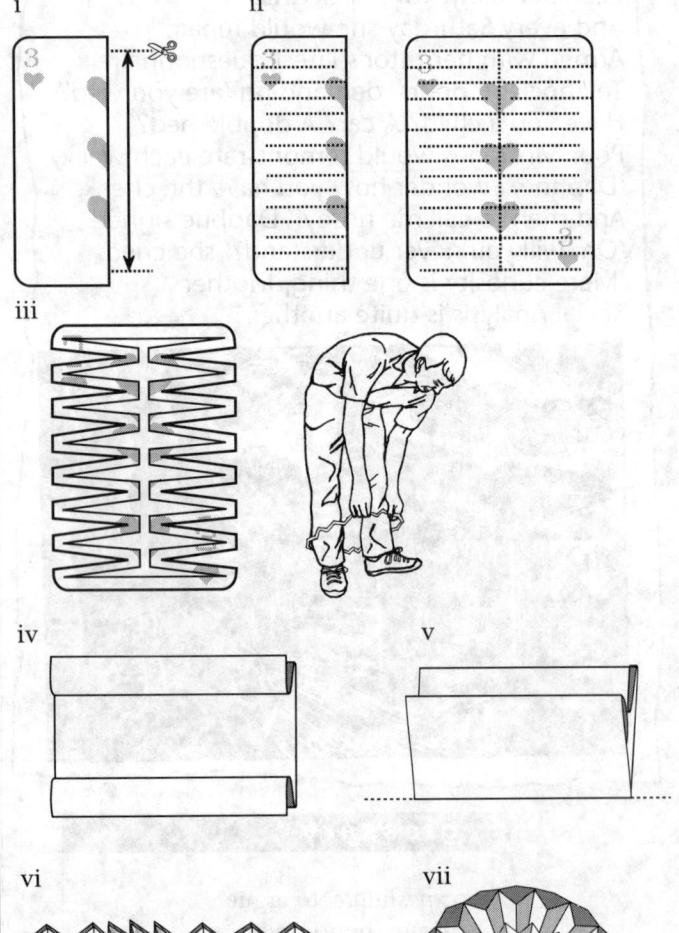

2 The instructions for these processes are mixed up below. Decide which instructions belong to which process, then put them into the correct order. The first one has been done for you.

How to climb through a playing card

1 [h] 2 ☐ 3 ☐ 4 ☐ 5 ☐

How to fold a napkin into a fan

1 ☐ 2 ☐ 3 ☐ 4 ☐ 5 ☐ 6 ☐

a Next form one inch pleats, back and forth, from end to end.

b Take any card from a deck that is damaged or incomplete.

c Lay the napkin on a table, and make a deep pleat at two opposite edges.

d Place the thinner end in a glass, and pinch down the inner fold of each pleat at the top edge, alternately at each side.

e Gently pull the ends apart and you will find the narrow band will open wide enough for you to step through it – and there are still three more suits in the deck into which you can step at will.

f To fold a napkin into a spectacular fan shape takes time, but the method is quite simple.

g Fold it in half lengthwise and cut a slit along the crease leaving a narrow strip at each end.

h All you need is to stretch your imagination and, of course, the playing card.

i Fold it in half with the pleats inside.

j This will fill out the final shape, and both glass and napkin are ready to place on the dinner table.

k Keeping it folded, cut slits at right-angles to the first one from the fold almost to the edge, then slits between those from the outer edge almost to the fold.

3 Match each picture in **1** with the correct instructions. Write the letter of the instruction by the picture.

4 The strength of the wind

The international scale used to describe the strength of wind was devised by Sir Francis Beaufort, a British admiral of the time of Nelson, and is known as the Beaufort scale. It rates wind from calm to hurricane.

Read the descriptions (not in order of strength) of the Beaufort Scale in terms of the wind and its effects inland. Rate them on the Beaufort Scale 0 – 12.

	Character of wind	Effects of wind inland	Scale
a	gale	twigs broken from trees, movement in open difficult	
b	light air	calm, smoke rises vertically	
c	gentle breeze	leaves and thin twigs move, pennants extended fully	
d	strong breeze	thicker branches move, whistling in telephone lines, umbrellas difficult to use	
e	light breeze	wind felt on face, leaves whisper, flags move	
f	storm	trees uprooted, major damage to houses	
g	fresh breeze	small trees in leaf begin to sway, white horses on lakes	
h	hurricane	severe destruction	
i	near gale	whole trees moving, resistance to movement against wind perceptible	
j	violent storm	widespread damage	
k	moderate breeze	paper and dust lifted, twigs and thin branches move	
l	strong gale	minor damage to houses (awnings and TV aerials)	

Language Focus

1 Fill in the blanks with the verbs in brackets in the passive.

America
America (**a**) .... (discover) by Christopher Columbus in 1492. In 1620 the Pilgrim Fathers arrived and the Atlantic coast of North American continued (**b**) .... (colonise) until the Declaration of Independence in 1776. In 1789 the first President, George Washington (**c**) .... (elect). In 1865 slavery (**d**) .... (abolish) when the South (**e**) .... (defeat) by the North in the Civil War. In 1929 the United States had become a world power, and the whole world (**f**) .... (affect) by the Wall Street crash of that year. Everyone who is old enough to remember knows exactly where they were on that fateful day in November 1963 when John F. Kennedy (**g**) .... (assassinate). His presidency had brought great hope to the American people. A sad contrast with the events of 1974, when President Nixon (**h**) .... (force) to resign over the Watergate Affair.

Writing

1 Look at the instructions you wrote out in the Reading section for **How to climb through a playing card**, and **How to fold a napkin into a fan**. Choose one of them and rewrite the instructions more formally by using the passive.

unit 9

Vocabulary

The Weather

1 Arrange these words in ascending order on the staircases.

a to rain   to drizzle   to pour   to bucket down   to pelt

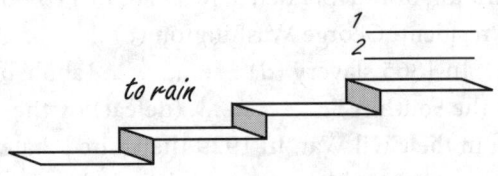

b shower   storm   deluge   downpour   cloudburst   thunderstorm

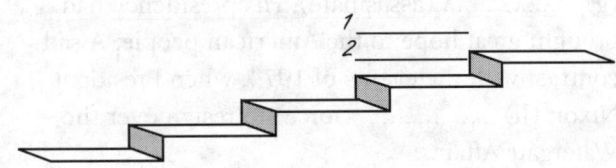

c breeze   gale   hurricane   wind   draught   gust   tyhoon

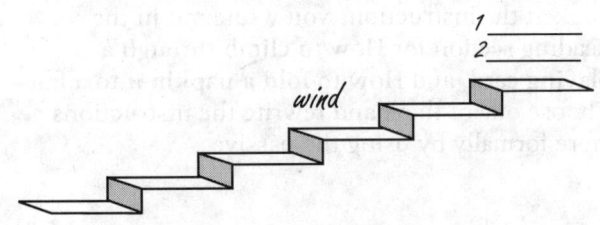

d warm   hot   scorching   boiling   mild   stifling

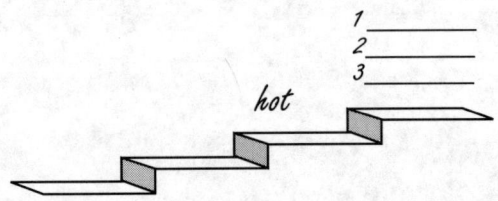

e cold   freezing   cool   icy   nippy   chilly   parky

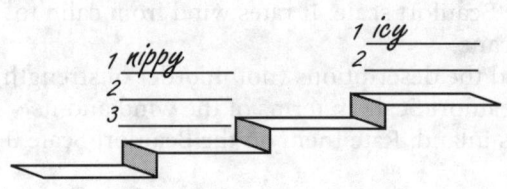

2 Try to make twenty words using only the letters of the word *climate*. You can only use each letter once in each word. For example, *team*.

40

Pronunciation

1 Homophones are words which sound exactly the same but are spelt differently.
Write homophones for the following words.

Example: bear   <u>bare</u>

a meet   ....
b farther   ....
c threw   ....
d their   ....
e great   ....
f board   ....
g caught   ....
h saw   ....
i war   ....
j find   ....
k sell   ....
l past   ....
m patience   ....
n guessed   ....
o stair   ....
p fair   ....
q where   ....
r dear   ....
s here   ....
t leek   ....
u heir   ....
v cent   ....
w feet   ....
x peal   ....
y die   ....
z four   ....

2

Say this tongue-twister five times as quickly as you can.

We surely shall see the sun shine soon.

Poem

1 The words below are taken from a poem by an American poet. Before you read the poem try to decide which words could refer to the wind and which could refer to the rain.

curved   swept   dry   fill   wells   warble
floods   lift   stir   cloud   seas   wet

     Wind   **Rain**

2 Read the poem and see which words refer to the wind and which words refer to the rain.

Like Rain it sounded till it curved
Emily Dickinson

Like Rain it sounded till it curved
And then I knew 'twas Wind –
It walked as wet as any Wave
But swept as dry as sand –
When it had pushed itself away
To some remotest Plain
A coming as of Hosts was heard
That was indeed the Rain –
It filled the Wells, it pleased the Pools
It warbled in the Road –
It pulled the spigot from the Hills
And let the Floods abroad –
It loosened acres, lifted seas
The sites of Centres stirred
Then like Elijah rode away
Upon a Wheel of Cloud.

glossary

spigot: small plug or pipe
Elijah: Old Testament prophet

unit 10

Looking into the future

'I never put off till tomorrow what I can possibly do the day after.'
Oscar Wilde (1856 – 1900), British dramatist, poet and wit.

Reading

1 Read *Twenty things I love to do* and carry out the instructions.

Twenty things I love to do

This is an activity to give you practice in discovering and clarifying your values, thereby helping you to choose your actions and plan them.

- List twenty things you love to do on the chart. They can be big or little things in your life; things appealing to the senses or more abstract pleasures; things you've always enjoyed, or relatively new experiences; things that you do or that others do for you; things done indoors or outdoors, at night or during the day, or in different seasons of the year. Be as specific as you can. Instead of listing *sports*, write *watching football on TV*. This is **your** list. Put down whatever comes to mind without judging it or wondering what others would think about it. There are no right or wrong answers. You may have a few more or less than twenty items.

- For each item, if it costs over the equivalent of £5 each time you do it, put £ in the first column.

- If you like to do it alone, write *A* in the next column, if you do it with others, write *P*, if you like to do it both alone and with others, write *AP*.

- Write *PL* in the next column if it requires planning.

- Write *N5* if it would not have been on this list five years ago.

- Pick the five you love most and rank them from 1 – 5 in order of preference.

- Write approximately how many days it has been since you last engaged in each activity.

	Activity	£	A-P	PL	N5	1-5	days
1							
2							
3							
4							
5							
6							
7							
8							
9							
10							
11							
12							
13							
14							
15							
16							
17							
18							
19							
20							

2 Look at these instructions on how to make a flow-chart.

Flow-charts are used to set out a sequence of actions and decisions as clearly and logically as possible. They are used in science, industry, commerce, and especially in computer programming. Making your own flow-chart can be fun, and improves your powers of logical thinking.

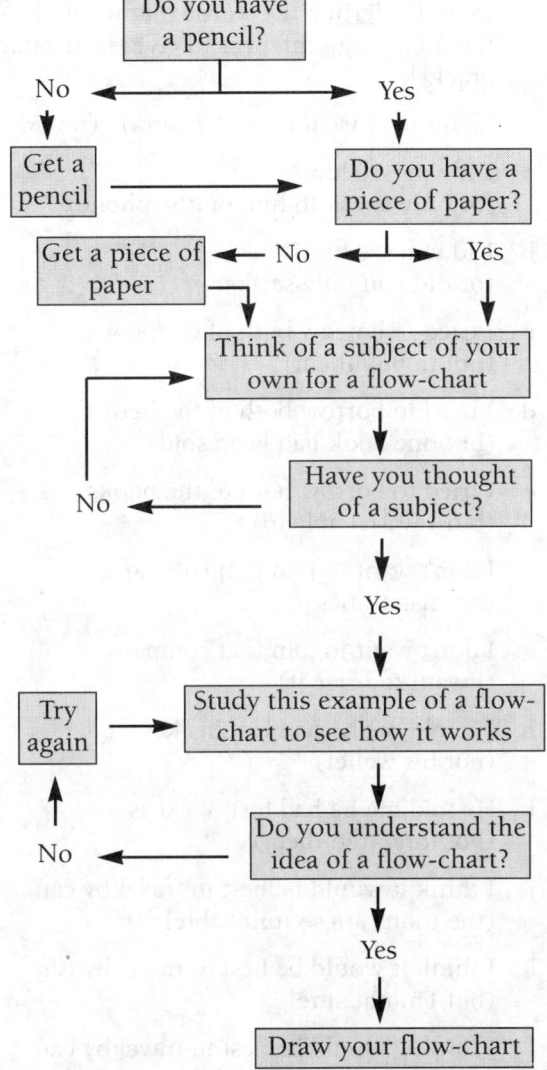

3 Choose one of your favourite activities in Reading **1** and put the information into a flow-chart. You can add anything else you think is relevant or helpful.

Writing

1 Write a paragraph about your favourite activity using the information you put in the flow-chart.

Language Focus

1 Underline the words that indicate the future in these sentences. The first one has been done for you.

a   I'm here <u>at Christmas</u>.
b   They'll be free on Tuesday.
c   His birthday's on Friday.
d   See you soon.
e   Won't you be living here next year?
f   This time next year we'll be travelling round Australia.
g   I may be there but I can't promise.
h   The day after tomorrow is my birthday.
i   I'm due to leave on Friday.
j   I'll have finished on Friday.
k   I could arrive earlier.
l   She should be here at 8.00.
m   I might leave this job.
n   Guess who's coming to dinner?
o   Is tomorrow Wednesday?
p   If you don't phone me I'll expect you at 2.00.
q   The train arrives at 7.00.
r   I'm going to watch a video.
s   I'm working in the morning and meeting my father in the afternoon.
t   I'm about to lose my temper.
u   How long are you staying?
v   It's unlikely I'll get the job.
w   Shall we meet at 6.00?
x   She's on the verge of a breakdown.
y   She's bound to be late. She always is.
z   There's a slim chance I'll get the job.

2 Write similar sentences about yourself using the words above that you underlined.

Vocabulary

Suffixes

-ish indicates 'approximately', for example, *We'll start 2 o'clockish* (We'll start around 2 o'clock).

-able means 'able to', for example if something is *washable* it means you can wash it.

-ful and its opposite *-less* can be used to form adjectives.

-proof means 'it can resist'. For example, *a bulletproof jacket* resists bullets.

-ment is added to some verbs to make nouns.

1 Put these words in the appropriate columns according to which suffix they take. Some words may fit into more than one column.

pain   break   meaning   young   drink   rust
home   idiot   develop   read   thought   rely
tune   red   colour   sound   water   avoid
worth   success   sound   announce   price
power   beauty   use   dust   enjoy   care
forget   hope   profit   manage   employ
agree   suit   govern   thirty   treat   depend

-able   -ful   -less

-ish   -proof   -ment

Pronunciation

Emphatic stress

1

Sometimes there is a particular word in a sentence we need to emphasise (stress) to make the meaning clear. Underline the words that would be stressed in the following sentences to give the meaning in the brackets.

Example: *I want to see Mr Brown.* (not Mrs Brown)

a   Did you see him?
    (or only speak to him on the phone)

b   Did you see him?
    (or did you only see her)

c   I tried to borrow both of the books.
    (not to buy them)

d   I tried to borrow both of the books.
    (but one book had been sold)

e   I tried to borrow both of the books.
    (but I wasn't able to)

f   I don't want to join that company.
    (my sister does)

g   I don't want to join that company.
    (I want to leave it)

h   He told me he had lost his keys.
    (not his wallet)

i   He told me he had lost his keys.
    (not forgotten them)

j   I think it would be best to travel by car.
    (the trains are so unreliable)

k   I think it would be best to travel by car.
    (but I'm not sure)

l   I think it would be best to travel by car.
    (my friend wants to go by bus)

m   I think you'll have to go to hospital.
    (but I'm not sure)

n   There were three hundred people.
    (not three thousand)

o   I can't speak French very well.
    (only a little)

Now say the sentences aloud, emphasising the words you have underlined.

2 🔊

Look at this dialogue between a man and his deaf aunt and underline the words you think Tom emphasises.

TOM: Well, this time next week I'll be in Morocco.
AUNT: Majorca, that's nice.
TOM: No, Morocco. In North Africa.
AUNT: I didn't know Morocco was in North America.
TOM: Not America, Africa.
AUNT: That's what I thought. What language do they speak?
TOM: French mostly. That's why I bought that teach yourself book.
AUNT: Do it yourself? Do what yourself?
TOM: I didn't say do it yourself. I said teach yourself. It's a really good book I got to brush up my French before I go.
AUNT: How are you getting there?
TOM: By plane.
AUNT: Train! That'll take a long time.
TOM: Plane. Why don't you switch on your hearing aid?
AUNT: There's no need. I can hear you perfectly well, and I don't want to waste the batteries.

3 Say the dialogue aloud.

Poem

1 This poem about space consists of unusual combinations of nouns and adjectives. Decide which of the adjectives might describe each noun. They may fit with more than one. Write a maximum of three adjectives for each noun.

Adjectives	Nouns
....	somersault
....	moon
....	headphone
....	spacesuit
....	beard
....	flood

growing   rough   crackling   golden
imaginary   hot   weightless   shining

2 Read the poem silently and compare your combinations of nouns and adjectives with those in the poem.

🔊

Spacepoem 3: Off Course
Edwin Morgan

the golden flood   the weightless seat
the cabin song   the pitch black
the growing beard   the floating crumb
the shining rendezvous   the orbit wisecrack
the hot spacesuit   the smuggled mouth-organ
the imaginary somersault   the visionary sunrise
the turning continents   the space debris
the golden lifeline   the space walk
the crawling deltas   the camera moon
the pitch velvet   the rough sleep
the crackling headphone   the space silence
the turning earth   the lifeline continents
the cabin sunrise   the hot flood
the shining spacesuit   the growing moon
   the crackling somersault   the smuggled orbit
   the rough moon   the visionary rendezvous
   the weightless headphone   the cabin debris
   the floating lifeline   the pitch sleep
   the crawling camera   the turning silence
   the space crumb   the crackling beard
   the orbit mouth-organ   the floating song

3 Read the poem aloud.

unit 11

Transport and Travel

'The only way of catching a train I ever discovered is to miss the train before.'
Gilbert Chesterton (1874 – 1936), English journalist, author, and critic.

Vocabulary

1 Make adverbs from these adjectives.

Example: moody *moodily*

a greedy .... f tidy ....
b angry .... g heavy ....
c noisy .... h hasty ....
d happy .... i lucky ....
e lazy .... j messy ....

2 Complete the sentences with an adverb. To help you, the first letter of each adverb has been given.

a If you say what you really mean you are speaking s...................
b A person with good manners behaves p...................
c A person who is ready to help does things w...................
d If you act without thinking you act h...................
e If you have a lot of energy you behave e...................
f If you are very interested in, and really like something you speak about it e...................
g If you are late you walk f...................
h If you do something now and again you do it o...................
i If you think about another person's needs and feelings you behave c...................
j If you are good at something you do it w...................

3 Make adjectives from these nouns. The first one has been done for you.

a difference *different* g violence ....
b silence .... h impudence ....
c excellence .... i evidence ....
d frequency .... j patience ....
e urgency .... k confidence ....
f absence .... l prudence ....

4 Complete the sentences below with a stronger adjective.

Example: *I'm very tired but he's absolutely exhausted.*

a I'm very hungry but he's absolutely ....
b I'm very poor but he's stony ....
c The weather here is cold but out there it's absolutely ....
d The weather here is hot but out there it's absolutely ....
e Our house is small but theirs is absolutely ....
f You may be rich but she's absolutely ....
g I'm angry but she'll be absolutely ....
h I got wet but he got totally ....
i My car is clean but his is absolutely ....
j Our house may be dirty but theirs is absolutely ....

46

Reading

1 Read this extract from a short story.

The Voyage — Katherine Mansfield

The Picton boat was due to leave at half past eleven. It was a beautiful night, mild, starry, only when they got out of the cab and started to walk down the Old Wharf that jutted out into the harbour, a faint wind blowing off the water ruffled under Fenella's hat, and she put up her hand to keep it on. It was dark on the Old Wharf, very dark; the wool sheds, the cattle trucks, the cranes standing up so high, the little squat railway engine, all seemed carved out of solid darkness. Here and there on a rounded wood-pile, that was like the stalk of a huge black mushroom, there hung a lantern but it seemed afraid to unfurl its timid, quivering light in all that blackness; it burned softly, as if for itself.

Fenella's father pushed on with quick, nervous strides. Beside him her grandma bustled along in her crackling black ulster; they went so fast that she had now and again to give an undignified little skip to keep up with them. As well as her luggage strapped into a neat sausage, Fenella carried clasped to her her grandma's umbrella, and the handle, which was a swan's head, kept giving her shoulder a sharp little peck as if it too wanted her to hurry . . . Men, their caps pulled down, their collars turned up, swung by; a few women all muffled scurried along; and one tiny boy, only his little black arms and legs showing out of a white woolly shawl, was jerked along angrily between his father and mother; he looked like a baby fly that had fallen in to the cream.

Then suddenly, so suddenly that Fenella and her grandma both leapt, there sounded from behind the largest wool shed, that had a trail of smoke hanging over it, *Mia-oo-oo-O-O!*

'First whistle', said her father briefly, and at that moment they came in sight of the Picton boat. Lying beside the dark wharf, all strung, all beaded with round golden light, the Picton boat looked as if she was more ready to sail among stars than out into the cold sea. People pressed along the gangway. First went her grandma, then her father, then Fenella. There was a high step down on to the deck, and an old sailor in a jersey standing by gave her his dry, hard hand. They were there; they stepped out of the way of the hurrying people, and standing under a little iron stairway that led to the upper deck they began to say good-bye.

2 Decide whether each statement is true or false. Where there is no statement, write one of your own that is either true or false as indicated.

		True	False
a	They went to the Old Wharf by bus.		
b	Fenella was wearing a hat.		
c	....	✓	
d	....		✓
e	Fenella was carrying a sausage.		
f	....		✓
g	The noise from the wool shed was the 'first whistle'		
h	....	✓	
i	....		✓
j	This extract is from a short story by Katherine Mansfield.		

unit 11

Language Focus

1 Complete these separate mini-dialogues between you and a fellow passenger (P) on a train.

a Ask the fellow passenger to help you put your luggage on the rack.
He/she agrees.
Respond.

You: ....

P: ....

You: ....

b Ask him/her if you can open the window.
He/she refuses and explains why not.
Respond.

You: ....

P: ....

You: ....

c Ask the passenger if you could look at his/her newspaper.
He/she agrees.
Respond.

You: ....

P: ....

You: ....

d Offer to help the passenger with his/her luggage.
He/she turns down the offer.

You: ....

P: ....

e The passenger asks you for a light.
Tell him/her you haven't got one.
He/she responds.

P: ....

You: ....

P: ....

f Ask him/her not to smoke as it's a non-smoking compartment.
He/she apologises.

You: ....

P: ....

g Offer to give him/her a lift from the station.
He/she accepts.

You: ....

P: ....

Writing

1 Write a letter to a friend who is going to visit your country for the first time. Give advice on what to pack, how to travel, where to stay and where to go.

2 Using the same information, write a short article for the travel page of a newspaper.

Pronunciation

Consonant clusters

1

These words all start with two or more consonants together. Practice saying them aloud.

a station stand stupid sting static staggering stammer stilts

b school scrape scale scamper scold screech scribble scream

c Spain space spill spend spoil sprint spread spend spot

d please plan plenty plain plant place platform play plural

e splendid splash split splatter

f blind blame bless blot blister blow blue bland blond bliss

g bright brown bring braces brilliant bronze breeze browse

h clever clean claim clown climb clan cling classify clear

i cream crease crisp crew crime crisis critic crown cross

j print praise promise prove propose property prevent protein

k fling flame fly flap fluid flute flower flow floor

l frame frighten freeze friend free fresh frequent fry frog

2

Say these tongue-twisters five times each as fast as you can.

Dressed in drip-dry drawers.
Please Paul, pause for applause.
Fresh fried flesh of fowl.
Three free flow pipes.

Poem

1 Add a verb to rhyme with each of the verbs below. (Use a dictionary to find the meanings of any words you don't know.)

Example: slide *glide*

sprawl	....	prance	....
strive	....	toil	....
sprinkle	....	beam	....
bound	....	gush	....
bubble	....	slap	....
rumble	....	twirl	....
batter	....	thump	....
beat	....	clash	....
spray	....	descend	....

2

This poem consists mainly of participles which give an impression of the sound and movement of something.
Read the poem twice. The first time silently, the second time aloud. Exaggerate the vowel sounds as much as possible.

The Cataract at Lodore — Robert Southey

Dividing and gliding and sliding,
And falling and brawling and sprawling,
And diving and riving and striving,
And sprinkling and twinkling and wrinkling,
And sounding and bounding and rounding,
And bubbling and troubling and doubling,
And grumbling and rumbling and tumbling,
And clattering and battering and shattering;
Retreating and beating and meeting and sheeting,
Delaying and straying and playing and spraying,
Advancing and prancing and glancing and dancing,
Recoiling, turmoiling and toiling and boiling,
And gleaming and streaming and steaming and
     beaming,
And rushing and flushing and brushing and gushing,
And flapping and rapping and clapping and slapping,
And curling and whirling and purling and twirling,
And thumping and plumping and bumping and
     jumping,
And dashing and flashing and splashing and clashing;
And so never ending, but always descending,
Sound and motions for ever and ever are blending,
All at once and all o'er, with a mighty uproar,
And this way the Water comes down at Lodore.

unit 12

Learning English Looking Backwards and Forwards

'A man never knows how to say good-bye; a woman never knows when to say it.'
Helen Rowland, American humorous columnist and author.

Reading

1 Match these riddles with their answers.

a Which trees do hands grow on? ☐
b What comes down but never goes up? ☐
c What goes up when the rain comes down? ☐
d What is a volcano? ☐
e Where does August come before July? ☐
f What two animals go with you everywhere? ☐
g What word is always pronounced wrong? ☐
h What tables can you eat? ☐
i What has teeth but no mouth? ☐
j Why are wolves like cards? ☐

Answers

1 Your calves
2 A mountain with hiccups
3 Palm trees
4 A Comb
5 Vegetables
6 The Rain
7 They come in packs
8 An umbrella
9 In the Dictionary
10 Wrong

2 Fill in the blanks in the following riddles.

a Q: .... do birds fly south in winter?
   A: .... it's .... far to walk.
b Q: .... is a river .... the letter 'T'?
   A: When it must be crossed.
c Q: .... is a fruit cake like an ocean?
   A: .... it's .... of currents.
d Q: .... is a bus .... a bus?
   A: When it turns .... a street.
e Q: .... is an empty purse always .... same?
   A: Because there's never any .... in it.
f Q: What animal can fly higher .... a house?
   A: All .... them. Houses .... fly.
g Q: .... did the boots say .... the cowboy?
   A: You ride, I'll go .... foot.
h Q: Why ....n't the bicycle stand up?
   A: .... it was .... tyred.
i Q: .... couldn't the pony talk?
   A: .... he was a little horse.
j Q: What horse is only found at night?
   A: A ....

Language Focus

1 Put the verb in brackets in the appropriate tense and form.

1 Now we (**a**).................... (work) on the last unit of this book. We (**b**).................... (use) it for a long time and (**c**).................... (work) very hard. In the first unit we (**d**).................... (have) (**e**).................... (introduce) ourselves to each other, and then we (**f**).................... (talk) about the things we (**g**).................... (like) and (**h**).................... (not like) (**i**).................... (do).

2 In the second unit we (**a**).................... (read) about traditions and festivals and (**b**).................... (listen) to people (**c**).................... (talk) about their cultures.

50

3 In the third unit we (**a**).................. (have) (**b**).................. (learn) how (**c**).................. (express) obligation and prohibition, and all the words we (**d**).................. (need) for that. One day we might (**e**).................. (need) (**f**).................. (apply) for a job in English, so we (**g**).................. (talk) about what we (**h**).................. (must) and (**i**).................. (must) not do when (**j**).................. (send) a letter of application and (**k**).................. (go) for an interview.

4 In the next unit we (**a**).................. (think) about what we (**b**).................. (do) when we (**c**).................. (be) children, and when we (**d**).................. (do) this we (**e**).................. (make) up stories.

5 In the fifth unit we (**a**).................. (read) about London restaurants which (**b**).................. (be) a bit unusual and we also (**c**).................. (focus) on food and recipes. We (**d**).................. (had) (**e**).................. (write) a recipe which we (**f**).................. (like).

6 In unit 6 we (**a**).................. (think) about crimes and criminals and we (**b**).................. (have) (**c**).................. (say) what other people (**d**).................. (say) in different words.

7 In the seventh unit we (**a**).................. (study) conditionals and (**b**).................. (read) an article about Mr Chan's house in Japan. If I (**c**).................. (live) there I (**d**).................. (feel) really claustrophobic.

8 Next we (**a**).................. (look) at education and we (**b**).................. (study) gerunds and infinitives. I (**c**).................. (not enjoy) (**d**).................. (do) that because it (**e**).................. (be) so difficult (**f**).................. (remember) which verbs (**g**).................. (take) which.

9 In unit 9 we (**a**).................. (subject) to the passive and we (**b**).................. (show) some of the differences between American English and British English. We also (**c**).................. (listen) to a funny tape about a bricklayer who (**d**).................. (hurt) by his pulley.

10 In unit 10 we (**a**).................. (think) about the future and what (**b**).................. (happen) and what changes there (**c**).................. (be). We (**d**).................. (decide) that in thirty years time many things (**e**).................. (change) a lot, and we thought about what we might (**f**).................. (do).

11 The eleventh unit (**a**).................. (call) *Transport and Travel* and we (**b**).................. (study) different interesting, complicated, new and old adjectives.

12 Finally in this last unit we (**a**).................. (revise) what we (**b**).................. (do) in the rest of the book and (**c**).................. (think) about what we (**d**).................. (do) in the future (**e**).................. (continue) (**f**).................. (learn) English.

Writing

1 Write a short report on your progress in English. Include any problems you have overcome, any problems you still want to work on, and your recommendations for your future studies. Write it in the third person as if you were your teacher writing a report on you.

unit 12

Vocabulary

Numbers

1 🔊

Write out this poem replacing the numbers and symbols (for example –) with the words they represent.

> **OIC**
>
> I'm in a 10der mood today
> & feel poetic, 2;
> 4 fun I'll just – off a line
> & send it off 2 U.
>
> I'm sorry you've been 6 o long;
> Don't B disconsol8;
> But bear your ills with 42de,
> & they won't seem so gr8.

2 The sentences below all include expressions containing numbers. Fill in the blanks with the correct numbers.

a He must be going somewhere very special. He's all dressed up to the ....s.

b It doesn't really matter which. It's .... of one and .... a .... of the other.

c You shouldn't jump to conclusions. You've put .... and .... together and made ....

d Why didn't you do it before. You always leave everything to the .... hour.

e I hardly ever see him. .... in a blue moon.

f I really don't trust her. She's so ....-faced.

g What's so special about that? They're .... a penny.

h I could hardly get a word in. He talked .... to the ....

Collective nouns

3 Complete each of these lists with a suitable word and then finish the sentence by adding the appropriate collective noun. The first one has been done for you.

a Forgery, arson, rape and ...*murder*...... are all ...*crimes*........

b A traitor, a blackmailer, a mugger and a .... are all ....

c Marks, francs, lire, and .... are all ....

d A president, a minister, an MP and a .... are all ....

e An aubergine, a courgette, a green pepper and a .... are all ....

f A, e, i, o, and .... are all ....

g Fast, happily, thoroughly, and .... are all ....

h Oak, poplar, larch and .... are all ....

i Primrose, daffodil, snowdrop and .... are all ....

j Go, teach, think and .... are all ....

Pronunciation

1 🔊

Words ending with -ate

If a **verb** ends in *-ate* the ending is pronounced /eɪt/ as in *plate*.

If an **adjective** ends in *-ate* the ending is very weak and pronounced /ət/.

Some **nouns** ending in *-ate* are pronounced /eɪt/ and some are /ət/.

Say the following aloud.

Verbs	Adjectives	Nouns
communicate	fortunate	carbohydrate
exaggerate	delicate	mandate
cultivate	moderate	graduate
investigate	private	chocolate
separate	separate	
discriminate	adequate	
create	accurate	
graduate	ultimate	

a   He communicated a very accurate mandate.

b   He investigated my private papers.

c   Now he's graduated he's going to do a post-graduate course.

d   It's difficult to separate all the separate pieces.

e   This has created a very delicate situation.

f   I've at last cultivated a moderate approach.

g   He exaggerated about my far-from-adequate income.

2

Put the words below into columns which have the same vowel sound.

hair   fare   sir   word   bear   bar   heard   wear   were   where   mayor   further   her   mercy   blur   party   fairy   started   clerk   work   stare   occur   cart   are   prayer   girl

Fur	Fair	Far
/ɜː/	/eə/	/ɑː/

3

Say this tongue-twister five times as quickly as possible.

How much wood would a woodchuck chuck if a woodchuck could chuck wood?

Poem

1   Categorise the words below into those that have pleasant or unpleasant associations for you.

friendship   pain   stillness   bitterness   paradise   chaos   together   bury   tremble   solemn

Pleasant	Unpleasant

2   Read the poem twice, the first time silently, the second time aloud.

On time for once   Brian Patten

I was sitting thinking of our future
and of how friendship had overcome
so many nights bloated with pain;

I was sitting in a room that looked onto a garden
and a stillness filled me,
bitterness drifted from me.

I was as near paradise as I am likely to get again.

I was sitting thinking of the chaos
we had caused in one another
and was amazed we had survived it.

I was thinking of our future
and of what we would do together,
and where we would go and how,

when night came
burying me bit by bit,
and you entered the room

trembling and solemn-faced,
on time for once.

key

unit 1
Language Focus

1 Answers will vary, but should be in these forms:
a past or past perfect simple or continuous
b present continuous c infinitive without *to*
d past participle e infinitive without *to*
f present perfect simple or continuous
g present simple h gerund (*-ing* form)
i *at* followed by gerund j *at* followed by gerund
k gerund l gerund m gerund or infinitive
n gerund o gerund or infinitive
p gerund or infinitive

Reading

1 (a) for (b) to (c) with
2 (a) than (b) about (c) by (d) on (e) of (f) of
3 (a) of (b) for
4 (a) with (b) of (c) from
5 (a) in (b) of (c) to
6 (a) than (b) as
7 (a) of (b) outside
8 (a) to (b) of (c) for (d) as (e) than (f) as
9 (a) of (b) in (c) of (d) at (e) on
10 (a) after (b) with

Vocabulary

a terrible / appalling awful bad okay / all right
  good wonderful / fantastic superb
b tired sleepy / dozy / drowsy shattered /
  exhausted / dead beat / all in
c damp wet dripping / soaking
  wet through / saturated
d peckish hungry starving / famished / ravenous

Pronunciation

1
/d/	/t/	/id/
managed	finished	hated
analysed	introduced	studied
adored	disliked	adapted
received	focused	reacted
advised	stroked	manipulated
attained	worked	depended
failed		pretended
diagnosed		
identified		
performed		
described		

2
odd ones out	other possibilities
your	shower tower
sour	draw for
food	look good

Poem

2 **He likes**: dictation, spelling tests, doing things, arithmetic
He doesn't like: painting, self-expression, dodging things, projects, modelling

unit 2
Reading

1 a 5 b 9 c 1 d 2 e 10 f 7 g 3 h 6 i 11
j 8 k 4

Language Focus

1 a I believe it's a real problem.
b This book does not belong to me.
c He's continually asking me the same question.
d You astonish me.
e It depends on my work.
f Do you know my brother?
g He's forever telephoning me.
h I'm cooking the lunch.
i Are you coming with us?

Pronunciation

2 a sealing b weight c tyre d tied e sail
f brake g caught h leek i bury j principle

4 a asleep b disagree c fleet d referee
e toffee f creeper g foresee h breezy
i absentee j beetle

Vocabulary

1
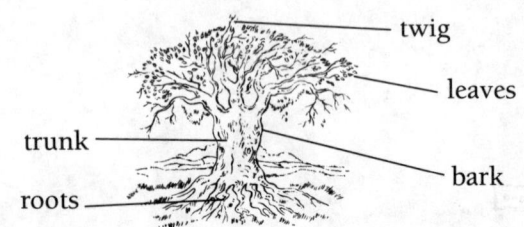

2 WELL DONE

3 a tea b thing c wells d liar e shoe
f earth g poles h rear i note j mood

54

unit 3

Language Focus

2 a He doesn't have to tidy rooms.
  b He would never need to wash his face.
  c He wouldn't need to do a thing.
  d He wouldn't need to do exams.
  e He wouldn't need to do a thing.

3 a You don't have to/don't need to/needn't be rich . . .
  b You don't have to/don't need to/needn't have a perfect English accent . . .
  c You must be able to/have to be able to speak . . .
  d You may/can leave . . .
  e You don't have to/don't need to/needn't join . . .
  f You can take time/may take time/you're allowed to take time out . . .
  g You must have/have to have . . .
  h You may/can park . . .
  i You should be/ought to be/must be loyal . . .
  j You mustn't/shouldn't/oughtn't to wear jeans.
  k You had to always wear . . .
  l You don't have to/don't need to/needn't wear . . .
  m You mustn't smoke . . .
  n You could smoke . . .
  o You don't have to/don't need to/needn't clock in.
  p You had to clock in.

4 a most b The more   the more c Most of d the most e the worst f the least g much more h the least i most of j much more

Reading

1 a hermit b confronted c eager d striving e urge f fray g disrupt h pursuit i ambiguous j a lack

2 Realistic d/5   Social b/3   Enterprising a/4   Artistic c/1   Conventional f/6   Intellectual e/2

Writing

Social people are best known for their interpersonal skills and interest in other people. Social work and counselling are possible careers and so is the organisation of others.

Enterprising people are characterised by high energy, enthusiasm, dominance and impulsiveness. They are well suited to occupations such as sales, politics, entrepreneurial business or foreign service.

Artistic people use feelings, intuitions and imagination, leading most obviously to the performing arts, writing, painting, and music.

Conventional people cope with life by following the rules and selecting goals approved of by society and customs. Accounting, office work and administration often suit them well.

Intellectual people like ideas, words and symbols. They are best suited to jobs in science, teaching or writing.

Vocabulary

1 a cunning b thin c tough d sweet e gentle f light g thick h drunk i poor j old

3 and Pronunciation 1

Adjective	Noun	Adverb	Verb
assertive	assertion assertiveness	assertively	to assert
reliable	reliability	reliably	to rely
determined	determination	determinedly	to determine
charming	charm	charmingly	to charm
adaptable	adaptation adaptability	(no adverb)	to adapt
authoritative	authority authorisation	authoritatively	to authorise
creative	creation	creatively	to create
persistent	persistence	persistently	to persist
weak	weakness	weakly	to weaken
persuasive	persuasion	persuasively	to persuade
tolerant	tolerance	tolerantly	to tolerate
considerate	consideration	considerately	to consider
patient	patience	patiently	
sincere	sincerity	sincerely	
enterprising	enterprise	enterprisingly	
honest	honesty	honestly	
ambitious	ambition	ambitiously	
courteous	courtesy	courteously	
loyal	loyalty	loyally	

Pronunciation

2 Hard *th* /ð/ bathe breathe smooth southern teething clothing northern soothe with leather

Soft *th* /θ/ bath south breath tenth teeth cloth north faithful birthday smith

key

Poem

1 reasonable *fair*   indifferent *not special*
to swear *to promise*   stench *bad smell*
good breeding *upbringing*   rancid *stale*
booth *kiosk*   tar *substance for making roads*
dumbfoundment *amazement*   assent *agreement*

3 Landlady: embarrassed, impatient, amazed, superior, confused, uncomfortable
Speaker: angry, amazed, inferior, nervous, ashamed

unit 4

Reading

1 to ladle *to spoon or serve*   to devour *to eat eagerly*
assiduously *diligently, carefully, thoroughly*
voracious *famished*   lots were cast *they did an activity to select one person*   pauper *poor*   to wink *to close one eye to signal to someone*   to nudge *to push someone with your elbow*   reckless *irresponsible*   temerity *courage*

2 Some possible answers: poverty, hunger, unhappiness, cruelty, fear

Writing

2   The teacher told his class that a short story must contain four principal elements. These elements were religion, society, sex and mystery, and they should appear in this order.
    He asked the class to write a short story in class, and to remember to include these four elements.
    After five minutes one of the boys put down his pen. The teacher read what he had written. He had managed to incorporate all the elements in only ten words. His story was, MY GOD (religion) said the DUCHESS (society) I AM PREGNANT (sex) WHO DUNNIT? (mystery).

Language Focus

1 (a) was born   (b) moved   (c) worked
(d) would pause/used to pause
(e) would trudge/used to trudge   (f) was
(g) hoped   (h) was trying   (i) was sent   (j) was
(k) was published   (l) was followed   (m) achieved
(n) poured   (o) died

Vocabulary

1 Someone Stole the Cat
The word *cat* fills each of the blanks to give the words:
cat-nap (little sleep)   cat   <u>cat</u>herine wheel (firework)   catch   cata<u>mar</u>an (sailing boat)   <u>cat</u>erpillar (insect that develops into a butterfly)   <u>cat</u>aract (waterfall)   cate<u>gor</u>ically (definitely)   cat<u>as</u>trophe (disaster)

2 a frog 7   b pig 4   c horse 11   d rat 6
e bull 12   f cows 9   g cat 3
h cat pigeons 10   i dog 13   j dog 1
k horse 8   l crocodile 5   m sheep 2   n wolf 4

4
a	ram	ewe	lamb
b	bull	cow	calf
c	drake	duck	duckling
d	stallion	mare	foal
e	cock	hen	chicken
f	gander	goose	gosling
g	stag	deer	hind
h	fox	vixen	cub
i	lion	lioness	cub

Pronunciation

2

rhyming words		some other possibilities		
scale	pail	tale	male	fail
site	might	fight	kite	white
square	prayer	share	wear	layer
cool	drool	fool	stool	pool
maim	frame	same	came	lame
sign	pine	fine	design	whine
dam	lamb	tram	jam	ham
cuff	tough	rough	enough	stuff
cow	bough	sow	prow	how
flew	through	true	crew	stew
try	high	pie	my	spy
roam	home	comb	foam	gnome
dumb	come	hum	chum	numb
pain	lane	rain	sane	pane
foul	owl	growl	howl	fowl
show	toe	dough	throw	so

Poem

1 Verse 1: wall nail hall pail foul owl
Verse 2: blow saw snow raw bowl owl

unit 5

Language Focus

1 Para 1: (a) the (b) – (c) – (d) – (e) – (f) a
(g) the (h) the (i) the (j) the (k) the (l) a
(m) the (n) a

Para 2: (a) the (b) – (c) – (d) some the
(e) the (f) the (g) – (h) – (i) a (j) the (k) a
(l) – (m) the (n) the (o) the (p) the (q) the
(r) the

Para 3: (a) the (b) the (c) the (d) the (e) the
(f) the

3
a ... a bomb explosion which hurt 50 people.
b ... a Picasso which has been sold for £100,000.
c ... interest rates which have increased by 1%.
d ... 16 protesters who have been imprisoned.
e ... a place which was hijacked in Kenya.
f ... the roads in N. W. Scotland which are flooded.
g ... share prices which have risen dramatically.
h ... the National Gallery which has been damaged by a hurricane.
i ... a Roman temple which has been discovered in Kent.
j ... the M25 which is blocked by an overturned lorry.

Pronunciation

1 fish and chips   bread and butter   eggs and bacon
milk and sugar   beef and onions
cheese and biscuits   ice and lemon

2 b marinated meat c chopped onions d diced carrots e mulled wine f mashed potatoes
g sliced bread h boiled water i ground coffee
j baked potatoes k sifted flour l grated lemon

Vocabulary

1 Possible answers

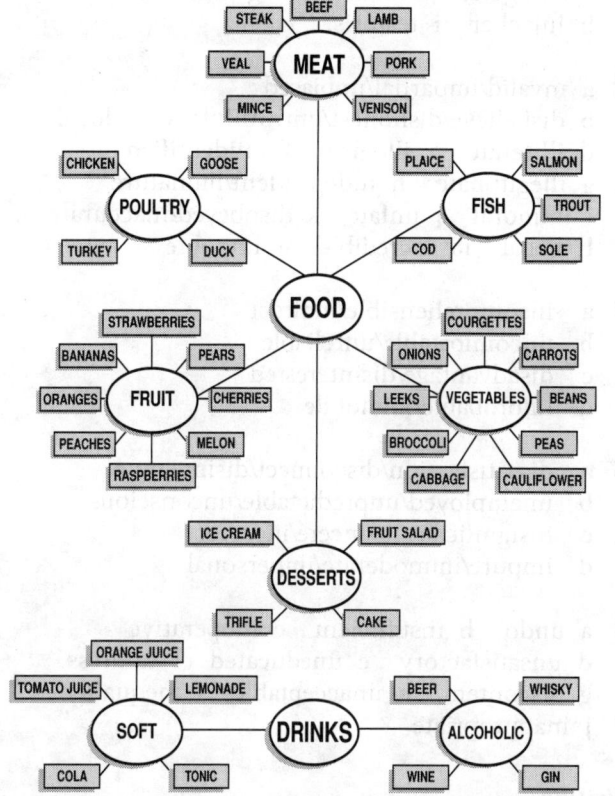

Reading

1 What time does *Absurd Person Singular* start?
How much are the tickets for *Blood Brothers*?
What is *Out of Order* about? Who wrote it?
Where is *Private Lives* on?
What days of the week is *Shirley Valentine* on, and what time does it start?
What's the telephone number of Her Majesty's Theatre?
Who wrote *The Phantom of the Opera*? What's it about?

unit 6

Vocabulary

1 a burgular b forger c murderer d imposter
     e smuggler f kidnapper g blackmailer
     h hijacker i terrorist

2 a invalid/impartial/unbiased
     b disbelieve/dishonest/untruthful c disloyal
     d illiterate e illogical f unidentified
     g illegitimate h independent/immature
     i immoral j unfair k disobeyed/inaccurate
     l illegal m incredible n impolite

3 a incomprehensible/indirect
     b uncomfortable/unreliable
     c disadvantage/disinterested
     d improbable/immobile

4 a dissatisfaction/disconnect/disintegrate
     b unemployed/unpredictable/unconscious
     c insignificant/insincere/incorrect
     d impure/immoderate/impersonal

5 a undo b insufficient c inoperative
     d unsatisfactory e uneducated f undress
     g discontent h unacceptable i inequality
     j inappropriate

Writing

1 D: Yes, I am.
     D: Yes, I was at a football match in Cardiff.
     D: My brother.
     D: John.
     D: With.
     D: Because my brother is at university there.
     D: Tourism.
     D: Tourism.

Language Focus

1 The Prosecutor asked the Defendant if he was called Martin Benson and lived in Oaten Hill Place, Newcastle. The Defendant confirmed this. The P. told him to tell the court where he had been on the afternoon of January 31, 1981. The D. replied that he was at a football match in Cardiff. The P. asked who he had gone with. The D. told him it was with his brother. The P. asked for the name of his brother and then queried whether John was spelt with or without 'h'. The D. told him it was without. The P. wanted to know why he had gone all the way to Cardiff for a football match, as it was a long way from Newcastle. The D. said it was because his brother is at university there. The P. asked what his brother is studying. The D. replied Tourism. The P. asked if he had said 'tourism' or 'terrorism'. The D. confirmed that he had said 'tourism'. The P. didn't believe him and remarked that it was a very interesting slip of the tongue.

Reading

1 If we suppose B is innocent, one of the twins must be guilty. This twin must have had an accomplice who couldn't be B because the twins always work together. Therefore it must have been the other twin. But this is impossible since the twins always work together, and one of the twins was in Dover at the time. Therefore B is guilty. And since B always works alone, both twins are innocent.

2 We know A is innocent. If we suppose B is guilty, we know s/he had once accomplice – (fact b) – either C or D. We know C always works with two accomplices (fact c), so C must be innocent. So if B is guilty, D is also guilty, and if B is innocent, D must be guilty. Therefore, D is guilty.

Pronunciation

1 végetable térrific consíderate cómfortable stationéry múrderer dífferent vocábulary scandálous séveral explánatory mónastery búsiness líterary désperate prósperous ínteresting díctionary oríginally náturally

1 Law there gravity stare air thin uncombed awake depravity square cards stifled repair way stair away thumbs suavity spare known crime.

2 odd ones out | possible other words
     a definite surprise | delight despise rewind
     b cough   muff | bluff   fluff   cuff
     c dear   prayer | care   dare   layer
     d pear   beer | cheer   near   mere

unit 7

Reading

1 a/5 b/2 c/6 d/3 e/1 f/4

2 a bad-tempered b a shoot growing from the main stem of a plant c to protect d someone/thing that destroys or devastates something e a verb, generally used for a bird, meaning *to sit* f a clever way of doing something g to cut grass h rough

key

Language Focus

1
a If we didn't spend so much time and money on the panda we could spend it on something more deserving.
b If ivy didn't have poisonous berries it wouldn't have such a bad name.
c If ivy didn't have a bad image, people wouldn't destroy it.
d If the seagull wasn't so adaptable it wouldn't have won the Special Award for Adaptability.
e If the robin didn't seem to be so friendly and approachable it wouldn't be on so many Christmas cards.
f If the llama could carry a person or give lots of milk it wouldn't have won the Least Useful Four-Legged Animal Award.

2
a House prices won't rise unless interest rates fall.
b The house market will stay dead as long as the inflation rate doesn't fall.
c I'll buy your house provided that I can sell mine.
d I'll buy your house on condition that I can move in next month.
e I would have bought your house but for the fact that the surveyor advised me against it.
f Supposing I bought your house, then I could walk to work every day.

Vocabulary

1 monk monastery   eskimo igloo
gypsy caravan   queen palace   soldier barracks
camper tent   a rich person mansion
a very poor person slum   artist studio

2 rabbit hutch   budgerigar cage   cow shed
horse stable   pig sty   dog kennel
fish aquarium

3 a sprint b march c stroll d limp e waddle
f dawdle g stride h toddle i strut j slouch

4 Suggested answer: hobble   dawdle / wander   stroll
walk / saunter   run   dash / rush   sprint.

5
a crawled (all the others mean *to jump*)
b strolled (the only word with a sense of relaxation)
c rushed (the only word with any speed)
d soared (the only word with an upward movement)
e paced (the only word which involves being 'on the ground')
f strode (the only word with purpose and speed)

Pronunciation

2
a *Make a Pig of Yourself* by Chris P Bacon (crispy bacon)
b *End of the Week* by Gladys Friday (glad it's Friday)
c *Who saw him leave?* by Wendy Go (when did he go?)
d *Sahara Journey* by Rhoda Camel (rode a camel)
e *Detective Stories* by Watts E Dunn (what's he done?)
f *Fitting Carpets* by Walter Wall (wall to wall)
g *The Winner* by Vic Tree (victory)
h *The Broken Window* by Eva Brick (heave a brick)
i *The Open Window* by Eileen Doubt (I leaned out)
j *Raincoats* by Anna Rack (anorak)
k *How to Make an Igloo* by S K Mow (eskimo)
l *There's a Hole in my Bucket* by Lee King (leaking)
m *The Olympics* by Arthur Letic (athletic)

unit 8

Vocabulary

1 a friend b appearance c receive d height
e beginning f developing g notable
h argument i attach j address k foreign

2 and Pronunciation 1
a exp<u>lore</u> / explor<u>a</u>tion   b <u>class</u>ify / classifi<u>ca</u>tion
c de<u>ceive</u> / de<u>cep</u>tion   d sub<u>scribe</u> / subs<u>crip</u>tion
e <u>hes</u>itate / hesi<u>ta</u>tion   f op<u>pose</u> / op<u>po</u>sition
g re<u>peat</u> / repe<u>ti</u>tion   h <u>spec</u>ify / specifi<u>ca</u>tion
i com<u>bine</u> / combin<u>a</u>tion   j <u>can</u>cel / cancel<u>la</u>tion
k con<u>trib</u>ute / contri<u>bu</u>tion   l <u>al</u>ter / alter<u>a</u>tion
m in<u>form</u> / infor<u>ma</u>tion   n sus<u>pect</u> / sus<u>pi</u>cion
o ex<u>plain</u> / expla<u>na</u>tion

Pronunciation

2 a lis̸ten b whis̸tle c lam̸b d deb̸t e autum̸n
f p̸sychology g w̸hole h w̸rite i righ̸t
j k̸nock k pal̸m l daugh̸ter m h̸onest n hal̸f
o coul̸d p wal̸k q Wed̸nesday r hand̸kerchief
s cup̸board t Chris̸tmas u foreig̸n v k̸nee
w plum̸ber x sig̸n y yac̸ht z c̸haracter

Reading

1 Verse 1: (a) to (b) in (c) to (d) to (e) up
(f) on (g) to (h) down (i) in
Verse 2: (a) to (b) to (c) to
Verse 3: (a) off (b) at (c) with (d) to
Verse 4: (a) at
Verse 5: (a) on (b) at (c) at (d) at
Verse 6: (a) through (b) for

key

Verse 7: (a) in (b) of (c) over or at (d) in (e) up (f) at (g) at
Verse 8: (a) over (b) at (c) but
Verse 9: (a) down (b) at (c) of (d) about (e) off
Verse 10: (a) as (b) but

Language Focus

1 a *of* + gerund b *on* + gerund c *of* + gerund
 d object + infinitive/or *between* + gerunds
 e *of* + gerund f *in* + gerund g infinitive
 h *with / of* + gerund i *of* + gerund j *for* + gerund
 k infinitive l *in / with* + gerund m infinitive
 n gerund o gerund p *in* + gerund

2 (a) moreover (b) furthermore (c) whereas
 (d) on the other hand (e) whilst

Poem

2 a some tea b another summer hat
 c it's idle, empty-minded and low
 d going for his beer e sociology

unit 9

Reading

2 How to climb though a playing card:
 1 h 2 b 3 g 4 k 5 e
 How to fold a napkin into a fan:
 1 f 2 c 3 i 4 a 5 d 6 j

3 (i) g (ii) k (iii) e (iv) c (v) i (vi) a (vii) d

4 a 8 b 1 c 3 d 6 e 2 f 10 g 5 h 12 i 7
 j 11 k 4 l 9

Language Focus

1 a was discovered b to be colonised c was elected d was abolished e was defeated f was affected g was assassinated h was forced

Writing

How to climb through a playing card

Use a card from a damaged or incomplete deck. The card is folded in half lengthwise and a slit is cut along the crease, leaving a narrow strip at each end. With the card folded, slits are cut at right-angles to the first one, from the fold almost to the edge. Then more slits are cut between those from the outer edge almost to the fold. The ends are gently pulled apart to produce a narrow band, wide enough to be stepped through.

How to fold a napkin into a fan

The napkin is laid on a table and a deep pleat made at two opposite edges. It is then folded in half, with the pleats inside. Next, one-inch pleats are made, back and forth, from end to end. The thinner end is placed in a glass, and the inner fold of each pleat is pinched down at the top edge, or at each side. This will produce the final shape, and both the glass and the napkin are then ready to be placed on the dinner table.

Vocabulary

1 a to drizzle to rain to pour to pelt / bucket
 b shower cloudburst downpour storm / thunderstorm deluge
 c draught breeze gust wind gale hurricane / typhoon
 d mild warm hot boiling scorching, stifling
 e cool nippy / parky / chilly cold icy / freezing

2 Some of the possibilities:
 me tea eat meat team lime clime time lame came tame cat mat at mile tile ale male tale mail tail ail it lit mite cite am clam aim claim ate late mate ice mice lice lie melt celt metallic

Pronunciation

1 a meat b father c through d there e grate
 f bored g court h sore i wore j fined
 k cell l passed m patients n guest o stare
 p fare q wear r deer s hear t leak u air
 v sent w feat x peel y dye z for

Poem

1 and 2
 Wind: curved swept dry
 Rain: fill wells warble floods lift cloud seas

unit 10

Language Focus

1 b 'll c on Friday d soon e won't/next
 f next year/I'll g may h the day after tomorrow
 i due to j 'll k could l should m might
 n 's coming o tomorrow p 'll q arrives at 7.00
 r going to s 'm working/morning/afternoon
 t about to u how long are v 'll w shall
 x on the verge of y bound z 'll

60

Vocabulary

1
-able	-ful	-less
breakable	painful	painless
drinkable	meaningful	meaningless
readable	thoughtful	thoughtless
reliable	tuneful	tuneless
avoidable	colourful	colourless
useable	successful	soundless
enjoyable	powerful	homeless
forgetable	beautiful	worthless
profitable	useful	priceless
manageable	careful	powerless
employable	forgetful	useless
agreeable	hopeful	careless
suitable		hopeless
treatable	*-proof*	
dependable	rustproof	*-ment*
governable	idiotproof	development
	soundproof	announcement
-ish	dustproof	enjoyment
youngish	waterproof	employment
reddish		agreement
thirtyish		management
		government
		treatment

Pronunciation

1 a see b him c borrow d both e tried f I
g join h keys i lost j car k think l I
m think n hundred o very well

2
TOM: Well, this time next week I'll be in Morocco.
AUNT: Majorca, that's nice.
TOM: No, <u>Morocco</u>. In North Africa.
AUNT: I didn't know Morocco was in North America.
TOM: Not <u>America</u>, <u>Africa</u>.
AUNT: That's what I thought. What language do they speak?
TOM: French mostly. That's why I bought that teach yourself book.
AUNT: Do it yourself? Do what yourself?
TOM: I didn't say '<u>do</u> it yourself'. I said '<u>teach</u> yourself'. It's a really good book I got to brush up my French before I go.
AUNT: How are you getting there?
TOM: By plane.
AUNT: Train! That'll take a long time.
TOM: <u>Plane</u>! Why don't you switch on your hearing aid?
AUNT: There's no need. I can hear you perfectly well, and I don't want to waste the batteries.

unit 11

Vocabulary

1 a greedily b angrily c noisily d happily
e lazily f tidily g heavily h hastily i luckily
j messily

2 a sincerely b politely c willingly d hastily
e energetically f enthusiastically g fast
h occasionally i considerately j willingly

3 a different b silent c excellent d frequent
e urgent f absent g violent h impudent
i evident j patient k confident l prudent

4 a famished / starving b broke c freezing
d sweltering / stifling / boiling e tiny / minute
f loaded / rolling in it g furious
h saturated / drenched i spotless j filthy

Reading

1 a false b true c possible answers: It was a starry night. Fenella was behind her father.
d possible answers: The Old Wharf was well lit. Her grandma walked behind her father. e false
f possible answers: Her grandma was carrying her umbrella. The men held their caps in their hand.
g true h possible answers: There were a lot of people on the gangway. Her grandma got on to the boat first. i possible answers: Her grandma got on to the boat last. There was a ramp up to the upper deck. j true

Language Focus

1 a You: Please could you help me put this case up on the rack?
P: Yes of course.
You: Thanks a lot.

b You: Do you mind if I open the window?
P: Well I'd rather not. I'm so cold.
You: Okay. Don't worry.

c You: Do you think I could have a look at your paper?
P: Yes of course.
You: Thanks very much.

d You: Can I help you with your luggage?
P: No. It's okay thanks.

e P: Have you got a light?
You: No, I'm afraid not.
P: All right. Never mind.

key

    f You: I'm sorry, but would you mind not smoking. This is a non-smoking compartment.
          P: Oh, I'm so sorry. I hadn't realised.

    g You: I've got my car at the station. Would you like a lift home?
          P: Oh that's very kind of you. Thanks very much.

unit 12

Reading

1 a 3 b 6 c 8 d 2 e 9 f 1 g 10 h 5 i 4 j 7

2 a Why because too **b** when like
     c Why because full (currants) **d** When not into
     e Why the change **f** than of can't
     g What to on **h** could because two (too tired)
     i Why because (hoarse) **j** nightmare

Language Focus

1 1 a are working b have been using
         c have worked d had e to introduce
         f talked g liked h didn't like i doing
     2 a read b listened c talking
     3 a had b to learn c to express d needed
         e need f to apply g talked h must
         i mustn't j sending k going
     4 a thought b used to do c were d had done
         e made
     5 a read b were c focused d had to e write
         f like
     6 a thought b had c to say d had said
     7 a studied b read c lived d would feel
     8 a looked b studied c didn't enjoy d doing
         e was f to remember g take
     9 a were subjected b were shown c listened
         d was hurt
   10 a thought b will happen c will be
         d decided e will have changed f be doing
   11 a was called b studied
   12 a have revised b have done c have thought
         d will do e to continue f learning

Vocabulary

1 Oh, I see
tender too for dash to you sick so
be disconsolate fortitude great

2 a nines b six half-a-dozen c two two five
     d eleventh e once f two g two
     h nineteen dozen

3   possible answers: collective nouns
     b thief   criminals
     c yen   currencies
     d chancellor   politicians
     e carrot   vegetables
     f u   vowels
     g completely   adverbs
     h oak   trees
     i tulip   flowers
     j sit   verbs

Pronunciation

2 Fur /ɜː/ sir heard were further her mercy blur work occur girl
Fair /eə/ hair fare bear wear where mayor fairy stare prayer
Far /ɑː/ bar party started clerk cart are